THE
GERMAN SOLDIER
IN THE
WARS OF THE UNITED STATES

3rd Edition

Joseph George Rosengarten

an imprint of Sunbury Press, Inc.
Mechanicsburg, PA USA

an imprint of Sunbury Press, Inc.
Mechanicsburg, PA USA

For information about special discounts for bulk purchases, please contact Sunbury Press Orders Dept. at (855) 338-8359 or orders@sunburypress.com.

To request one of our authors for speaking engagements or book signings, please contact Sunbury Press Publicity Dept. at publicity@sunburypress.com.

FIRST DISTELFINK PRESS EDITION: March 2021

Set in Adobe Garamond | Interior design by Crystal Devine | Cover design by Lawrence Knorr | Edited by Lawrence Knorr.

Publisher's Cataloging-in-Publication Data
Names: Rosengarten, Joseph George, author.
Title: The German soldier in the wars of the United States / Joseph George Rosengarten.
Description: Third trade paperback edition. | Mechanicsburg, PA : Distelfink Press, 2021.
Summary: The various contributions of persons of German descent to the American military cause from colonial times through the 19th century are documented. This newly edited and revised third edition includes illustrations.
Identifiers: ISBN : 978-1-620065-30-3 (softcover).
Subjects: HISTORY / Military / United States | HISTORY / Europe / Germany | HISTORY / United States / Colonial Period (1600-1775) | HISTORY / United States / Revolutionary Period (1775-1800) | HISTORY / United States / Civil War Period (1850-1877).

Product of the United States of America
0 1 1 2 3 5 8 13 21 34 55

Continue the Enlightenment!

In Memory of

Adolph G. Rosengarten,
Major 15th Pennsylvania (Anderson) Cavalry,

Born in Philadelphia, December 29, 1838
Killed in battle at Stone River, Tennessee, December 29, 1862

Contents

Preface & Acknowledgments

The substance of the following pages was read before the Pionier Verein at the hall of the German Society in Philadelphia, April 21, 1885. It was printed with some changes in the *United Service Magazine* of New York, in the numbers for June, July, and August 1885, and it was translated and printed in German in full in the *Nebraska Tribune*, in successive issues, between June 20th and October 27, 1885—the last number being a supplementary article by the translator, Fr. Schnake, on the German Soldiers of the Border States. It was subsequently published in a pamphlet of forty-nine pages by J. B. Lippincott Company, Philadelphia, for the Pionier Verein. That edition is exhausted, and in reply to numerous applications showing interest in the subject, it is now reprinted with many corrections and considerable additions. For these, the author is indebted most of all to the *Deutsche Pionier* of Cincinnati and the editor, H. A. Ratterman, the best authority on all subjects concerning the Germans of the United States—and among others to Mr. F. Melchers, of the *Deutsche Zeitung*, Charleston, South Carolina; Mr. Herman Dieck, of the *German Demokrat*, Philadelphia; General Lewis Merrill, U.S.A.; Colonel John P. Nicholson, Dr. J. de B. W. Gardiner, U.S.A.; Prof. O. Seidenstricker, of the University of Pennsylvania, and Mr. George M. Abbot, of the Philadelphia Library—his *Bibliography of the Civil War in the United States* is indispensable for a student of our military history. Whatever there is of merit or interest in these pages is largely due to the assistance thus liberally given. With further aid in the way either of corrections or additions, which will be gladly received and gratefully acknowledged, the author of this sketch hopes that he may hereafter be enabled to make it better worth the interest of the reader and the importance of the subject.

J. G. R.

PHILADELPHIA, April 21, 1886
532 WALNUT STREET

Foreword

By Lawrence K. Knorr

Many things about this book have surprised me. I was first exposed to it thanks to my late great uncle, Arthur Dundore Graeff, Ph.D., who used it as a reference for his dissertation *The Relations Between the Pennsylvania Germans and the British Authorities, 1750–1776*. I found a copy of the expanded second edition on an antiquarian book site and ordered it. When it arrived, I was impressed with J. G. Rosengarten's compact but detailed presentation of the subject. I was reminded of what the great historian George Bancroft had said about the Pennsylvania Germans, as recounted in the preface of Graeff's book, "Neither they nor their descendants have claimed all that is their due." Rosengarten, writing thirty or more years after Bancroft, was trying to claim a portion of that German contribution. While Rosengarten's pride in his German heritage is evident at times in his text, he provided a balanced and accurate account of the contributions of these many martial participants.

Next, I was surprised when researching the author's background. I had not stumbled upon Joseph George Rosengarten in my research, despite writing about the American Revolution and the Civil War—at least that is what I thought. When reading his obituary (see the Afterword), I realized he had been an aid to my cousin, General John Fulton Reynolds, who was killed on the first day at Gettysburg. My memory had failed that I had included snippets about "Joe" Rosengarten in a previous book on the general over a decade ago.

Here is what I had forgotten. On Tuesday, June 30, 1863, Captain Rosengarten, Sergeant Charles Veil, and other aides were with General Reynolds at the Moritz Tavern, six miles south of Gettysburg. The following morning, sensing the upcoming battle, at 9:15 A.M. on July 1, Reynolds sent Rosengarten to warn Gettysburg citizens to stay in their homes. A half-hour later, while his troops were marching double quick to Seminary Ridge, Reynolds paused briefly on the Emmitsburg Road to watch the troops' advancement. There he saw Rosengarten and noticed his eyeglasses were dirty. Reynolds joked with him, asking if the townspeople had thrown mud at him for telling them to stay in their houses. Then the 1st Corps band marched past playing "The Girl I Left Behind Me."

Forty-five minutes later, at 10:30 A.M., Reynolds was shot and killed almost instantly while placing troops near the Chambersburg Road. Sergeant Veil attended to him, surprised that he had fallen from his horse despite lacking any perceptible wound. But the general had been shot through the neck, severing his spinal cord. He was paralyzed and quickly asphyxiated. Veil and Rosengarten helped remove the general from the field, taking him into town. There, they searched for a coffin but weren't successful. They settled for a box that was not quite long enough and knocked the bottom out so the general's boots would fit. They escorted the box in an ambulance to Union Bridge, Maryland, where, that evening, the general was placed in a proper coffin. The body then went to Baltimore to be embalmed and then to Philadelphia, where it was taken to the general's sister, Mrs. Landis, at 1829 Spruce Street. The final leg was by train to Lancaster, where the body arrived accompanied by aides and the family at 11:30 A.M. on July 4. Flags were at half-mast, and crowds filled the street as the general's funeral cortège moved slowly to the cemetery. He was then laid to rest.

Said Captain Joseph G. Rosengarten about Reynolds: "Impetuous without rashness; rapid without haste, ready without heedlessness; he liked better to be at the head of a compact corps than to command a scattered army."

So, in a weird twist of fate, I was surprised to realize this gentleman had been a friend of my cousin's, had served with him during the Civil

War, had witnessed his death, and had cared for his body when he fell. I suddenly felt indebted to Captain Rosengarten for his actions on the field. Suddenly, this book was also about my family.

However, Rosengarten's most amazing surprise is the career he led as a historian and a philanthropist. This was surprising to me because I first checked his biography at Find-a-grave, and it only mentioned his rank in the military and vital information. Fortunately, the American Philosophical Society had published a comprehensive obituary upon his passing in 1921. I will let you read about that in the Afterword and not repeat that here. And no, it is a complete coincidence we are publishing this edition on the 100th anniversary of the author's death—another weird surprise about this whole project. Suffice to say; Joseph George Rosengarten was a great human being. He seemed to be of the highest character, incredibly unselfish and devoted to his scholarship and many friends. It's almost like he is guiding this project from above, or someone else is on his behalf because he never drew attention to himself.

Sunbury Press has thus published this third edition, not because of the connections to John Reynolds, but because it remains an essential scholarly work for researchers of Pennsylvania German and early American military history. The book has been lightly edited to improve the narrative. The manuscript has been broken into chapters, and the lists have been moved to their appropriate sections. We have also included the author's biography in the Afterword and inserted over fifty period paintings, lithographs, and photographs. Lastly, you will find a new index at the back.

Introduction

The Germans' share in the wars of the United States is by no means limited to that of the Rebellion. From the very outset of their settlement in the country, they always stood ready to take their place in its defense. On the borders of what was then the West, the early German immigrants were steady in their support of the British flag against their hereditary enemies, the French. This was natural enough, for many of the Germans who first came to this country did so to seek refuge from the French invaders. They rode rough-shod over their humble homes in the districts of Germany devastated by French soldiers. Even among those who came here to find a new home in which they could worship God in their own way, while they sympathized with the Quakers in their doctrine of not bearing arms voluntarily, the German blood did not easily accommodate itself to the doctrine of non-resistance, and when they could not make friends of the Indians by peaceful means, the German settlers did not hesitate to take up arms in defense of their homes. The Germans of Pennsylvania and New York responded freely to the summons to defend their new country against the French and their allies, the Indians. They freely gave their men and their means to the cause of liberty in the war of the Revolution. They took a full share in the War of 1812 and the Mexican War. Finally, wherever the Germans were strongest in number, they were represented in even more than proportionate strength in the forces raised for the Union's defense. From New York and Pennsylvania, they went forth in great strength in regiments and individually. They saved Missouri to the Union. Ohio and Illinois and Indiana and Wisconsin and Kansas may well point with pride to their German citizens as foremost in doing their duty in war and peace. The story of their achievements in war is a subject on which little has hitherto been said.

Chapter One

French and Indians

The Germans from the Palatinate had been scattered on the frontier, facing the Indians and the French in New York and Pennsylvania. The early settlers in South and North Carolina and Georgia were also largely recruited from the Germans. They, too, had still another hostile force to meet, that of the Spanish troops and Indians, whose masters were unwilling to see their territory threatened and diminished. The good Moravians gave up their settlements in Georgia rather than fight and thus lost the fruits of some years of labor in their schools and churches. The sturdy Protestants from the Palatinate were not afraid to take up arms to defend their own homes. In a very short time, the British government, which had brought them here as an act of benevolence, found a good return in the German settlers' services as peacemakers with the Indians, and when necessary, as soldiers against the French and the Spanish and their native allies. There was, indeed, quite a characteristic jealousy of them on the part of their unwarlike neighbors in Pennsylvania. Not a little of the hostility that marked the early German settlers' treatment in New York was due to their sturdy indifference to those, both Dutch and English, the great landowners, who would have controlled them and used them as feudal serfs. They acknowledged their allegiance to the crown and gladly served it. They refused to submit to the tyranny of great landlords, and on that account, they soon left New York to find permanent homes under the Penns' kindlier sway.

Pennsylvania made Conrad Weiser colonel of a regiment of volunteers from the county of Berks. Governor Morris, in 1755, gave him command over the second battalion of the Pennsylvania regiment, consisting of nine companies. In defense of the borders against the Indians and the French, forts were built by the German settlers above Harrisburg, at the forks of the Schuylkill, on the Lehigh, and Upper Delaware. The Honorable Daniel Ermentrout, in his address at the German Centennial Jubilee in Reading in June 1876, described the Tulpehocken massacre in 1755, just after Braddock's defeat, the barbarities perpetrated in Northampton County in 1756, and the attack on the settlements near Reading in 1763. Against these forays, the Germans under Schneider and Hiester made a stout resistance. As early as 1711, a German battalion, mainly natives of the Palatinate, was part of the force, a thousand strong, to take part in the expedition to Quebec. While the Quakers of Pennsylvania kept the government from exerting its full strength, the Germans stood up stoutly for their homesteads despite their peace principles. Berks, Bucks, Lancaster, York, and Northampton were then the frontier counties, and from them came the men who filled the German regiments and battalions of the Revolutionary War. The sufferings inflicted on the German settlers were not without their influence in inspiring their descendants with the patriotism which made them good soldiers both in the Revolution and in the war of the Rebellion.

At the outbreak of the old French war, the British government, under an act of Parliament passed for the purpose, organized the Royal American Regiment for service in the colonies. This force was to consist of four battalions, of one thousand men each. Fifty of the officers were foreign Protestants, while the enlisted men were to be raised principally from among the German settlers in America. The immediate commander, General Bouquet, was a Swiss by birth, an English officer by adoption, and a Pennsylvanian by naturalization. This last distinction was conferred on him in compliment and as a reward for his services in his campaigns in the western part of Pennsylvania, where he and his Germans atoned for the injuries that resulted from Braddock's defeat in the same border region.*

The first colonel of the regiment was Lord Loudoun, and the four battalions were commanded by Stanwix, Duffeaux, Jeffereys, and Provost. Lord Howe was commissioned a colonel in 1757 when he was first ordered to America. The regiment itself still exists as the Sixtieth of the line of the British army. Bouquet himself died in 1765 at Pensacola, just after receiving the thanks of the Assembly of Pennsylvania for his victory at Bushy Run in 1763. The Germans of his force were due much of the credit of this action, making amends for the disaster of Braddock's defeat. A chaplain of this regiment, who shared in its operations at Louisburg and on the frontiers, the Rev. Michael Schlatter, died at Chestnut Hill, Philadelphia, in 1790, in the enjoyment of a pension from the British government, although he had proved himself a good patriot in the Revolutionary War. His descendants were well known as successful merchants in Philadelphia, while his memory is honored by a biography giving an account of his varied services to the church.

But from the Germans of Pennsylvania, there was an influence among the Indians more potent in saving the country from desolating border warfare than soldiers or fortifications. While the French were striving to make the Indians their allies in war, the Germans, and especially the Moravians, were working successfully to convert the savages into peaceful Christians and make them good neighbors, useful and obedient to the authorities, and a strong defense against the inroads of their more savage brethren influenced by the French. The Moravians sent their members out to preserve peace; their knowledge of the Indians and their languages, their intercourse, and intermarriages had secured the confidence of the untutored savages. Parkman, in his last work, *Montcalm and Wolfe in the French War of 1759*, describes at length the mission undertaken by Christian Frederick Post as envoy to the hostile tribes on the distant

---

* One of the best evidences of the interest taken in this organization is the sermon preached in Christ Church, Philadelphia, by the Rev. Dr. William Smith, which was printed at the request of the colonel and officers.

Ohio.* The Moravians were apostles of peace, and they succeeded to a surprising degree in weaning their Indian converts from their ferocious instincts and warlike habits. Post boldly presented himself among those who were still savage, and his first reception was by a crowd of warriors, their faces distorted with rage, threatening to kill him. Soon after, the French offered a great reward for his scalp, but Post, undaunted, declared to the Indians the coming of an army to drive off the French, and in return, received the promise of the warlike savages to keep the peace. After a conference at Easton, Post again went on a mission of peace to the tribes of the Ohio. The small escort of soldiers that attended him as far as the Allegheny was cut to pieces on its return by a band of the very warriors to whom he was carrying his offers of friendship. His overtures were accepted, and the Delawares, Shawnees, and Mingoes ceased to be enemies. The English soldiers failed by force of arms to accomplish what the German missionary had successfully attained. Thus, the work of the Moravians in their quiet home at Bethlehem had enabled their representative to gain the friendship and alliance of the Indians and to weaken the force of the French and proportionately strengthen that of the English, and this was in no small degree an important factor in the final overthrow of the French in America.

In Kapp's *History of the Early German Settlers of New York*, we find the first German soldiers' names, those who bore arms in defense of their hard-won homesteads against the French and their allies, the Indians. Among them were the Weisers, father and son. The elder, John Conrad, born in Württemberg, came to this country a few years after his native village was burned by the French in their invasion in 1693, and died in Pennsylvania in 1746, where he and other German settlers found refuge from the unfair treatment of the wealthy New York landowners. Conrad Weiser, his son, born in 1696 in Germany, came, with his father, as a boy to New York, and after a brief experience of border-life with the

---

* Frederick Post was a German Moravian, who, as early as 1761, settled in what is now Bethlehem Township, Stark County, Ohio, where he built a blockhouse and cleared a few acres of forest, and established a mission settlement. The family of Heckewelder joined him there, but later settled at Gnadenhütten in Tuscarawas County. The site of the former is marked by a few remains of the old block-house.

German settlers west of the Hudson, lived with the Indians long enough to be their fast friend, and to serve as their intermediary with the whites, helping thus to preserve the peace amid hostile influences. He died near Reading in 1760. As lieutenant-colonel of a Pennsylvania regiment, he shared in the hardships of the "old French war" and secured from the allied Indians an affection and respect which stood his fellow-Germans in good stead in later years. His daughter was the elder Muhlenberg's wife, the first of that name to come to this country, and the mother of General Muhlenberg of Revolutionary fame.

As early as 1711, the elder Weiser had led his German countrymen in an expedition to Canada in defense of the English against the French; and the younger Weiser, in 1737, boldly went out among the wild tribes of native Indians and successfully brought them to make peace with the new settlers. In 1748 he penetrated the unknown country west as far as Ohio. In 1754, he united the friendly Indians in a strong alliance, which greatly resisted the French intrigues and invasions.

During the Revolutionary War, while many of the Germans of New York were serving in the army, their homes and neighbors were exposed to the attacks of savage enemies, French and Indians rivaling one another in cruelties. The German settlers and their families defended themselves with real courage. The story of their heroic deeds well deserves the lasting record that Kapp has secured in his interesting volume. The border warfare of what was then Western New York showed that among the Germans there were many stout hearts and strong hands ready to defend their lives and protect their families. Each home was a block-house and every fort a gathering-point, yet the English were as bitter in repressing the liberty-loving Germans as ever the French had been in attacking them for their loyalty to England. Even when the war ended, it was with a sacrifice of lives and property that fell heavily on the German settlers. All this, however, was a training and experience that helped to make them devoted patriots and earnest in their readiness to sacrifice everything in defense of their newly acquired liberty and independence. From the same counties came many regiments into the army that helped to defend and preserve the Union. Although the distinctive German characteristics were less marked in New York than in Pennsylvania, still a military history of New York in the Rebellion, whenever it is written, will show that the Germans, descendants of the early Pfaslzers and Rhinelanders, who had settled in New York in the early part of the eighteenth century, were fully alive to the patriotic demand made upon them in the middle of the nineteenth century.

In 1728, the first conflict in Pennsylvania took place between Germans and Indians at Manatawny. In 1755, after Braddock's defeat, the Indians attacked the Moravian settlements, and they ravaged all the frontier counties. Franklin himself headed a regiment in Pennsylvania's defense, in which many Germans served, and he gave them hearty praise for their bravery. When another outbreak occurred in 1763, Bouquet, with his regiment of Royal Americans, officered as well as manned by Germans, put it down. The Germans of Charleston, South Carolina, organized in 1775 a Fusilier Company, which served through the Revolution and is still in existence. In Georgia, many of the early German settlers enlisted under General Wayne in the Revolutionary army.

Chapter Two

Revolution

The German soldier has gone through all the phases of history in our brief experience of war. In the Revolution, the Hessians became a by-word, and yet they were rather the victims of political evils than willing partisans. Not the least of Friederich Kapp's great services to both the country of his adoption and that of his nativity is his series of admirable works on the German soldiers of the Revolution, on the one side, his account of the dealings in them as mercenaries, and on the other, his lives of Steuben and De Kalb. Much of his material has supplied that for later authors, notably Green and Lowell. Von Elking has furnished the story of Riedesel's life, the commander of the German forces in the British army. The *Memoirs of Mme. Von Riedesel* will always be read with interest as a picture of the time of the Revolution, both in Germany and in America.

The material for a statistical account of the German forces engaged in America has been found in the well-ordered and well-preserved archives of the various German states from which they came. For our War of the Rebellion, such data are not easily attainable. The story covers too vast a field to be briefly told. The method of raising troops in the separate states obliges an inquirer to examine each state's printed records. These are so voluminous and so unsystematic that it is almost impossible to get at the facts of the soldiers' nativity serving in their organizations. Indeed, there remains to be a history of the part of New York in the war, and in those bulky volumes of war records of states already printed, it is hard to say which is the least satisfactory on this point.

The Seven Years' War made Germany's name and its great leader, Frederick, popular throughout the colonies. Town, village, and wayside inn displayed the well-known sharp features and high shoulders as a sign, and the "King of Prussia" was a favorite name for taverns—then of more importance than today—on all the high-roads between the great towns. Steuben was one of Frederick's veterans, and as such, he was heartily welcomed when French officers of high rank were coldly received. His zeal, ability, and success were shown in the provincial troops' improved discipline and instruction. He was so good a soldier that he knew how to use the material at hand and make good soldiers and good officers of what had hitherto been an undisciplined mass. Steuben's Regulations long remained the manual of the United States Army and its militia. It was not only that he made the army successful in the field, but the discipline he had introduced so effectually cultivated the sense of duty and subordination that a weak and impotent Congress, which had utterly failed of its duty to provide for its soldiers, was still able to disband an injured and irritated army peacefully. That he spent the rest of his life waiting for justice is not fairly compensated for by the posthumous honors paid his memory since his death, and the debt of gratitude that America owes to Steuben can never be fully discharged.

Much has been said and written in disparagement of the German mercenaries serving in the British army in the war of independence. It must be borne in mind that in England itself, the wickedness of thus hiring men against their consent was sharply denounced. Holland and Russia refused to accept the tempting offers of Great Britain. King George, himself a German sovereign, mildly protested against thus using his Hanoverian troops. Frederick the Great sternly forbade the enlistment of any of his subjects or permission to any of the petty German princes to take their soldiers through his territories to ports of shipment to England for America. Schiller stigmatized the trade in men in his *Kabale und Liebe*, while Kant went still further and embraced the American colonist's cause with all the energy of his great intellect. Klopstock and Lessing spoke in the same strain, although in lower tones. Frederic Kapp puts the total of twenty-nine thousand one hundred and sixty-six as the number furnished by Brunswick, Hesse-Cassel, Hanau, Waldeck, Anspach, and Anhalt, and of these only seventeen thousand three hundred and thirteen returned to their native country. How many of the remainders stayed in their new home to become American citizens' fathers cannot be easily ascertained. Yet, it is more than a tradition that in Pennsylvania, in Maryland, in Virginia, in North Carolina, wherever there were German settlers ready to aid the newcomers, the sick, the wounded, the stragglers, the deserters, all found protection and a welcome, which insured them prosperity and a better livelihood than they had left behind them. Their number has been roughly estimated at considerably over ten thousand.

Many Germans settled in the colonies before the Revolution, who cast their fortunes with the young republic and shared in the struggle that secured independence and union.

The German Battalion was raised agreeably to a resolve of Congress of May 22, 1776, four companies in Pennsylvania and four in Maryland, to which was added a ninth company by the resolve of July 9, 1777. The officers were: Lieutenant-Colonel, Ludwick Weltener; Major, Daniel Burckhart; Captains, Jacob Bunner, Peter Boyer, Charles Baltzel, William Rice, Bernard Hubley, Christian Myers, Michael Bayer; Captain-Lieutenant, Philip Schrauder; Lieutenants, John Weidman, Martin Sugart, Jacob Gremeth, Jacob Cramer, Godfrey Swartz, Marcus Young, David Morgan; Ensigns, John Weidman, Henry Shrupp, David Desenderfer, Henry Spech, Jacob Raboldt, Christian Glichner, William Prux, Henry Hehn.

An independent corps of one hundred and fifty men were raised by the resolve of December 5, 1776, of which the officers were: Captains, John Paul Schott, Anthony Selim.

In Henry's account of Arnold's campaign against Quebec, 1775 (Albany, Munsell, 1877), is a reference to the company of riflemen commanded by Captain William Hendricks, from Cumberland County, Pennsylvania, "an excellent body of men, formed by nature as the stamina of an army, fitted for a tough and tight defense of the liberties of their country." Hendricks "was tall, of a mild and beautiful countenance, his soul was animated by a genuine spark of heroism." In the same attack in which General Montgomery fell, he was killed at Quebec on the 1st of January, 1776, and the two heroes were buried side by side. Provost Smith, in his oration on Montgomery, speaks with unstinted praise of the Pennsylvania riflemen. Their funeral was marked by the British officers with every mark of honor. Of Hendricks's company, raised on the west side of the Susquehanna, scarcely a dozen names have been rescued from oblivion. Of the flower of the country, brave, ardent, and patriotic, and nowise daunted by the sufferings of the Arnold campaign, nearly all of those who returned safely from it served again in the Revolution. He is spoken of with equal praise by Thayer in his *Journal of the Invasion of Canada in 1775*, edited by Stone, published in Providence, Rhode Island, in 1867.

In Harris's *Biographical History of Lancaster County* (Lancaster, 1872), there are many names of its German settlers and their descendants who served as soldiers, with honor to themselves and credit to the race whence they sprang.

In Hamersly's *Dictionary of the Army*, and on the register of the army for 1784, there are the familiar names of General Steuben, inspector-general, and his aide-de-camp, Major William North, and that of Major Continental Artillery, Sebastian Bauman, captain New York Continental Artillery Company, 1776, brevet lieutenant-colonel, 1787.

The following hitherto unprinted letter of De Kalb, from the unrivaled collection of Ferdinand J. Dreer, Esq., of Philadelphia, is so characteristic of that hero, in its manly refusal to accept military precedence to Lafayette, that it is well worth publication, as showing the noble nature of the man:

BETHLEHEM, 18 Septr. 1777

SIR—I have been ever since I had the favour your letter by Mr. Secretary Thomson, in a very uncertain and fluctuating

Situation of mind, between the desire of serving in your Army, and the apprehension of blame from home. But Congress and your Esteem do me too much Honour, not to accept your late proposals, if they will grant me Several points I think essential to my tranquility and entire satisfaction. 1st. That I may be at Liberty to give up my Commission if in answer to the account I will send to France of my proceedings here and my behaviour towards those officers that came over with me, in case they were to exclaim against my stay, in any way that could be hurtfull to my reputation and honour.

2nd. As to the offer made to me by the Ministry of Mr. Thomson to have my Commission done of an older date than Marquiss de la Fayette's. I would decline it and have my Commission of the same day with his. That it may be in my power to show my regard for his friendship to me, in giving him the Seniority over me in America, in order, too, not to disgust him.

3rd. That Congress will be pleased to grant to Chev. Dubuysson, a Commission as Lt. Colonel with only the pay as a Major, or as my aid de Camp.

4th. That they will please to make provision for said Chev. Dubuysson of having the assurance of a Pension of 1200 Livres French money or fifty Louis d'ors to be paid in France for life if he serves this and next Campaign, and which they will augment at pleasure if he serves longer and they are satisfied with his having done his duty according to time and circumstances.

5th. That if Congress are disposed to do anything of that kind for myself it shall be done at their own terms and pleasure. The only thing I could wish in that respect, would be to have the favour bestowed on my Lady and children in case I died in the Continental Army or any other way while in their service.

On said Conditions I am ready to join the army as soon as possible and to go directly to Philadelphia from Lancaster, where I will wait for a Resolve of Congress, by Chev. Dubuysson, bearer of this.

Another observation I think necessary in regard to the immediate Command of a Division. General Washington has perhaps friends or deserving officers to whom he would give the preference, in such a case I should be sorry my coming in did in the least cross or prevent his dispositions in this and any other respects. I will gladly and entirely submit to his Commands and to be employed as he shall think most convenient for the good of the Service. If my second aid de Camp I am to chuse, chanced to be a foreigner, I should be glad some provision was made for him after leaving the service, in proportion to his rank as a Major.

I depend for the Settling of all these matters to the Satisfaction of all parties, on the friendship you are so kind to profess for me, and of which I have already so many proofs. These new obligations cannot increase the respect and high Esteem with which I have the Honour to be,

Sir,

Your most obedient,

Humble Servant,

BARON DE KALB

COLONEL RICHARD HENRY LEE,

Member of Congress

This is endorsed:

Com^d to B^d War

18th & 23rd Sept. 1777, acted upon.

From the same treasure-house of original material for history comes the letter from Steuben, written in French, from which the following is an extract:

Dear Friend

I have received your two letters of the 12th and 20th February—I would rather have seen you in person. I am infinitely obliged to

you for your news, for every thing which occurs in the army is
of interest. I am infinitely sorry for your account of Col. Bruchs
and Major Gils and would be glad to help them. To lose such
an officer as Bruchs would be a real misfortune. I have already
spoken of it to the President of Congress et je parlerai au bon
Dieu et au Diable. I would move Heaven and Earth to prevent it.
We are waiting for news from Gibraltar and Charlestown, as the
Jews wait for the Messiah. I have bet a hat on the fall of Gibraltar,
but I am afraid I shall win only a night cap. Our papers are full
of epigrams, abuse, and dreams of the late Mr. de Galvan on the
American army—his friends want to immortalize him. Let me
know if North has decided to go beyond Boston, for in that case I
fear much — but no, I won't fear anything. I hoped to present my
compliments to Mrs. Washington en route when your last letter
reported that she had gone. I would like to see you in my hermit-
age—where I am better quartered than since I came to America. I
rarely go into the city, but my friends come to see me in my cottage. I receive visits from European Grandees, such as the Prince
de Guimené, of the house of Rohan—who claim to be next after
the Bourbons of France. The Duc de Lauzun, the Comte de
Gillon, have both been here too. Our American Grandees are too
busy with great affairs to pay visits, but I have no pretensions, for
I have paid no visit except to the President of Congress, nor will
I. Yesterday I was at a supper and ball given by M. de la Luzerne
to the newly married Major Moore and his wife—there were
eighty persons, and among them many pretty women…. My fate
is not yet decided. I have just written to Congress to demand a
Committee, to which I can submit my uncomfortable situation.
I get no pay, rations or forage, and I live on money I borrow to
pay my marketing. My case is one of 'to be or not to be,'—I am
ready for anything. The Secretary of War will find it no harder
to replace me than the Adjutant-General, whose position he
offered to several persons of my acquaintance. 'Let him go' is the
favorite phrase of our Secretaries nowadays. I saw Robert Morris

yesterday—he seems more affected by the conditions of the army than anybody. I hope that after the 1st of January, not only will the subsistence of the officers be regularly paid, but that it may be increased. Say to them that no matter what happens, nothing can prevent me from being their advocate....I cannot deal with Lincoln, he has done me more harm than he thinks, but I don't want to be anybody's enemy, not even his. There are some people who are dangerous only as friends, and he is one of them, so it is prudent for me to treat him with indifference. I was not the aggressor, I sought his friendship, and if he had honored me with his confidence, my advice would have been better for him than that of his friend Cornel.... The Prince de Guimené wants to make the acquaintance of the General in chief—he said so to me, and if my finances do not prevent, I will go with him. Although he is only a Midshipman on the Frigate, he is a young man of the highest nobility in France—a grandson of the Prince de Soubise, who is Marshal of France. I give you warning, so that in case he comes, his air *of a little wild boy* may not prevent you showing him the consideration due to his birth. But what nonsense to talk this way in a Republic. My respects to the General.

STEUBEN

BELISARIUS HALL
Nov. the 26th

The register for 1789 gives captain 1st Infantry David Ziegler (late captain 1st Pennsylvania Continental Infantry). In the Indian border warfare between 1788 and 1795, a leading figure was David Ziegler, whose story is typical of that many of our early German soldiers. Born in Heidelberg in 1748, he served in the Russian campaign against the Turks under Catharine until the conquest of Crimea brought peace. He settled in Lancaster, Pennsylvania, in 1775. As adjutant of a Pennsylvania regiment, more than half made up of Germans—the second to enlist under Washington for the war—and as senior captain of the 1st Pennsylvania Continental Regiment, he won great praise. Later, he raised a company for war against the Indians in the West, took part in Clark's expedition, and was with General Harmar in 1790 and with St. Clair in 1791, in command of a battalion of regulars. He was made major and temporarily assigned command of the army for six weeks but was led to resign and was the first mayor of Cincinnati, where he died in 1811.

The army list for 1805-6 has Captain Artillery Michael Kalteisen, distinguished in connection with the Charleston (South Carolina) Germany company. Michael Kalteisen was born at Wachtelsheim, Württemberg, on the 18th of June 1729; in 1762, he was established in business in Charleston, South Carolina, where a large German population had already gathered. In 1766, with fifteen of his countrymen, he established the German Friendly Society of that city. By the time of the Revolution, it counted a hundred members and was well-off enough to advance two thousand pounds to the state for defense against the Crown. On the 12th of July, 1775, he set on foot the plan of a German military organization, which under the name of the German Fusiliers, by 1776, counted over a hundred Germans in its ranks. Its captain was Alexander Gillon, first lieutenant Peter Bouquet (brother of the general of that name), second lieutenant Kalteisen, ensign Gideon Dupont. From the day of their organization, they proved themselves true and ardent patriots. In 1779 it took part with the Continental forces under Lincoln and the French squadron under D'Estaing, in the siege of Savannah, having its captain, Scheppert, killed in the same assault in which Pulaski fell. The first captain, Gillon, had been made captain of the South Carolina fleet in 1779 and sent to France to buy three frigates. The Prince of Luxemburg gave him one for three years, guaranteeing its safe return and a fourth share of all prize money. He finally led a squadron of eighty sail and took the Bahamas. He left a son who, in 1817, was a member of the Fusiliers. Kalteisen died in 1807, and the hall of the German Society, with its tablet in his memory, was destroyed by fire in 1864. The Fusiliers, however, still exist, and the German Society still perpetuates the useful charity set on foot by him.

Of the Continental Army's general officers, the Germans were John De Kalb, F. von de Woedtke, F. W. A. Steuben.

In the pages of that excellent and useful journal, *Der Deutsche Pionier*, the organ of the society established under that name to preserve everything that relates to the history of the German settlers in this country, are found many records of the Germans who served the cause of American liberty, both in the Revolutionary War and in that of the Rebellion. Herkimer in New York and Muhlenberg in Pennsylvania are names that will long preserve the memory of the first German soldiers' services in defense of their adopted country. The Continental Army records show that in almost every regiment, there were Germans, and in those of Pennsylvania, whole regiments, battalions, and companies organized, officered, and filled with Germans, who did good service for their country. In the then western wilderness of Kentucky, Daniel Boone, with others like himself of German birth or descent, did their share in securing American liberty in their new home. In Virginia, North and South Carolina, and Georgia, there were many German settlers. Many went into the patriot army, sharing hardships and contented with helping to secure the final establishment of American independence as their full reward. In Gustav Körner's *Das Deutsche Element in den Vereinigten Staaten*, Cincinnati, 1880, there is a graphic account of the Germans from 1818 to 1848, with frequent reference to the earlier, as well as the later, Germans who took a distinguished place among the soldiers of the young republic in its first Revolution, and in its subsequent wars. Herkimer, Lutterloh, and Weissenfels in New York, Muhlenberg in Pennsylvania, Michael Kalteisen and his associates in the German Fusilier Company of Charleston, South Carolina, the oldest military organization of the country, established in 1775, are among those who were the first German citizens by their sacrifices and their services to secure the right to a place in the home of their adoption.

Friedrich Heinrich Baron von Weissenfels was the friend and companion of Washington, Steuben, and De Kalb, and his name deserves to be rescued from oblivion. Born in Elbing, Prussia, in succession to a line of soldiers (his father was major in the Swedish army), he served in the Silesian war under Frederick the Great, and, like Steuben, won at the hands of that royal soldier his decoration and order; in 1756 he entered the English service to take part in the old French war, was made an officer in the Royal American, the Sixtieth of the line, took part in the attack on Fort Ticonderoga, and the capture of Havana in 1762. He was at Wolfe's side when he fell at Quebec and served in the same regiment as St. Clair. Put on half-pay at the close of the war, he settled in New York, married a widow Bogart there, and had Steuben and Van Courtland as his groomsmen. As soon as the colonies began the Revolution, casting aside all thought of his own interest, he offered his services to the Continental Congress; was made captain of a regiment organized in New York in 1775, and was brigade-major at Quebec with Montgomery and Worster. In 1776 he was made lieutenant-colonel in command of the 3rd Battalion of the 2nd New York Regiment of the line. He was soon promoted to be colonel, serving at White Plains, Trenton, the capture of Burgoyne, and Monmouth. In 1779 he was second in command under Sullivan in an expedition against the Indians. He was distinguished for his gallantry and was honored by Washington and Congress with many marks of grateful acknowledgment. He died in New Orleans in 1806, poor in purse but rich in glory. His only son died in 1798, in Alexandria, Virginia, his widow in 1818, and his daughter in 1856. He was the first vice-president of the German Society of New York, with Steuben as its president. He was one of the original members of the Society of the Cincinnati, and his fellow Germans in that organization deserve to be chronicled here to show the appreciation of their share in the great work of securing the American republic's independence.

These original members were:

- Major-General Steuben, who died in 1795
- Colonel Henry Emanuel Lutterloh, a President of the Germany Society of New York
- Colonel Nicholas Fish, of New York
- Colonel Frederick von Weissenfels, of the 2nd New York Regiment
- Major Sebastian Bauman, died in 1803, of the 2nd New York Artillery Regiment

- Captain Henry Ticbout, died in 1826, 1st New York Regiment
- Captain George Sytez, 1st New York Regiment
- Lieutenant Peter Anspach, 2nd New York Artillery Regiment
- Lieutenant Henry Demler, 2nd New York Artillery Regiment
- Lieutenant Joseph Freilich, 2nd New York Regiment
- Lieutenant Michael Wetzel, 2nd New York Regiment
- Lieutenant John Furmann, 1st New York Regiment
- Lieutenant Carl Fr. Weissenfels, 2nd New York Regiment
- Captain-Lieutenant Peter Neslett, New York Artillery
- Captain-Lieutenant Peter Jaulmann, Sappers and Miners, died in 1835

This list is of the German members of the Society of the Cincinnati in New York alone, and no doubt on the rolls of the Society in other States there will be found many other Germans whose names belong to the roll of soldiers distinguished for their services in the war of the Revolution.

In Seidensticker's admirable and exhaustive *History of the German Society of Pennsylvania*, there is a brief mention of the services of the Germans of Philadelphia in the patriot cause. In May 1776, Congress organized a German regiment of companies from Pennsylvania and Maryland—the Pennsylvania companies were five in number and those from Maryland four. One of the Philadelphia companies was commanded by Colonel David Woelpper, an old soldier. He had served in Germany under Frederick the Great and in the old French war under Washington. Hausegger first commanded the German regiment, and it served with credit in Muhlenberg's brigade throughout the Revolution. Other German companies were raised at that time, and many Germans served in various arms of the service. The fines and penalties imposed on the German citizens of well-known rebel principles are all recited in Seidensticker's history, showing how strongly the German element in and about Philadelphia adhered to the patriot cause even at the time the British held the city. In Mr. H. M. Jenkins's *History of Gwynedd*, there is a similar collection of evidence about the stout adhesion of the Germans of Montgomery County to the rebel side. He tells the story of one of their number charged with the serious offense of giving information to the enemy and finally escaped severe punishment on the merciful ground that he was a weak politician—a plea that would cover many offenses in our day and generation.

John Paul Schott, the commander of a battalion in Armand's legion, was born in Prussia in 1744, served as a cadet, became adjutant of Prince Ferdinand of Brunswick, came to America in 1776, was authorized to raise an independent company of German dragoons, led the right wing of Hand's brigade in Sullivan's army, in 1779, in the attack on the Five Nations, and commanded the forts in Wyoming Valley to the close of the war. He filled a variety of civil offices afterward, dying in Philadelphia in 1829.

Major Barth van Heer led Washington's mounted bodyguard, which consisted of fourteen officers and fifty-three men, nearly all Germans. The 1st Continental Regiment of Pennsylvania was commanded by Colonel John Philipp de Haas, who was born in 1735, came to America in 1750, was an ensign in the French war, became a brigadier-general in 1777, took part in the expedition to Canada, and served with credit to the close of the war.

Among the French allied army sent to the help of the struggling colonies were many Germans, and the investigation of H. A. Ratterman, editor of the *Pionier*, attests both their number and influence. It will be found in *Volume XIII* of that journal (1881), on pages 317, 360, and 420. Colonel Esebeck commanded a regiment, "Zweibrücken" (the German equivalent for the French "Deux Ponts"). In Force's *Archives*, many of the details of others are given. At the time, it was a matter of arrangement between neighboring and friendly princes, how many of the men of one country should enlist in the army of another. France had troops from the Rhine Provinces, Baden, Bavaria, Württemberg, Anspach, and Switzerland. With the Zweibrücken Regiment came the two princes of the name, Major Esebeck in command and Captain Haake. A battalion from Trier served in Custine's regiment, one from Elsass, in the Bourbonnais, a large number were in Lauzun's cavalry regiment, and an Anhalt regiment assisted in the siege of Savannah. Among the German officers in the French service were Count Fersen, chief of staff of Rochambeau, besides his adjutant, Von Closen, and his chief of artillery, Gau. Count von Stedingk commanded the Anhalt regiment and, like his friend Fersen, belonged to the old Pomeranian nobility, although both afterward died in the Swedish service.

At Yorktown, the Germans in the American army fought for a time against the Germans under the English flag, and the commands were given on both sides in German. A detachment of Germans placed the French flag on the walls of Yorkton after its capture. Among the prisoners were countrymen of the troops put over them as a guard, and many met as old friends and neighbors. When Tarleton tried to force his way out of the lines, it was with the German cavalry under Ewald, and they were met and repulsed by the Germans under Armand. Ratterman's estimate that eleven thousand German soldiers remained in this country after the war may well be credited with recruits from both sides. With the Germans in the Pennsylvania brigade of Muhlenberg and the Maryland brigade of Gist, the German regiments in the English service soon made friends and found new homes. Indeed, the Anspach regiment, two days after the capitulation, offered their services as a body. Elking gives a list of twenty-eight officers of the Brunswick regiment who either remained or returned here after the war to settle.

In the *History of the Early Settlement and Indian Wars of Western Virginia*, by Wills de Hass (Wheeling and Philadelphia, 1851), at page 344, is a brief biographical sketch of Lewis Wetzel, a typical borderer, a brave and successful Indian fighter, and the right arm of the settlers in their almost ceaseless war with the natives. His father was one of the first settlers on Wheeling Creek and was killed in 1787 by Indians, sacrificing his own life to save his comrades. From that time, the son, then almost twenty-three years of age and already well trained by his father, devoted himself to avenging his life. At twenty-five, he enlisted under General Harmar, commanding at Marietta. In the army, he shot an Indian, was arrested, escaped, and reached home despite prison, guard, and fetters. An attempt to recapture him was given up out of fear of a counter-rebellion against the United States troops, and when he did get into their hands, General Harmar promptly released him. He went to New Orleans, was arrested, and released a broken man, yet he was long active in leading new settlers and purchasers through Western Virginia's trackless forests until he died in 1808. The name is perpetuated in Wetzel County, West Virginia.

However, the early German name seems to have passed through numerous variations—Whetzell, Whitzell, Watzel, and Wetzel—but of its German derivation, there can, of course, be no doubt. The Poes, too, who figure in this border history, were sons of German settlers from Frederick County, Maryland. The elder Frederick Poe, who moved west in 1774, and died in 1840 at the age of ninety-three, was, like his younger brother, Andrew, a backwoodsman in every sense of the word. Shrewd, active, and courageous, they fixed their abode on the frontier of civilization, determined to contest inch by inch with the native Indians their right to the soil and their privilege to live. Their hairbreadth escapes and bold adventures remain even now among the legends of their early homes and, fortunately, are preserved in the pages of the local historian. As late as 1846, there was found at the mouth of the Kanawha one of the leaden plates suitably inscribed, bearing date 1749, and asserting France's claim to the region watered by the Ohio River and its tributaries, and others were found at Venango and Marietta. Washington's expedition with the Virginia troops in 1754 first made this region familiar to the colonists, and settlements soon began. From Pennsylvania came some of the German Dunkards, who hoped to practice the peaceful doctrines of their Ephrata brethren, but with them came others more willing to fight than to pray, preferring to take land by force rather than by purchase. Braddock's campaign, with its disaster, only served to make the region better known to the Provincial troops, and from them came the best settlers in the region thus opened. The fate of the Christian and Moravian Indians settled at Gnadenhütten, Schönbrunn, Salem, and Lichtenau, massacred in cold blood, is a permanent blot upon the leaders of that inexcusable raid. It was terribly revenged in the utter failure of the next attack in 1782.

General George Weedon, really Gerhard von der Wieden, was born in Hanover, served in the war of the Austrian Succession, 1742 to 1748, was distinguished for his performance at the Battle of Dettingen, served with Colonel Henry Bouquet in Flanders, came with him as a lieutenant in his Royal American Regiment, and served with it in the old French war, in the capture of Fort du Quesne, and the campaign against the Indians. The war over, he settled in Fredericksburg, Virginia, then largely populated by Germans, and when the Revolution broke out became captain and later on lieutenant-colonel of the 3rd Virginia Militia, colonel of the 1st Virginia Continental, and finally, on February 24, 1777, brigadier-general, taking a leading part in the battles of Brandywine and Germantown; he left the service for a time, then in 1780 re-entered it under Muhlenberg, and commanded the Virginia militia at the siege of Yorktown.

Armand's legion was originally organized by Nicholas Dietrich Freiherr von Ottendorff, a Saxon nobleman, a lieutenant under Frederick the Great, who came to this country with Kosciuszko, and became major, commanding an independent corps of light infantry. It was subsequently reorganized as cavalry under Armand, Ottendorff became lieutenant-colonel, and his adjutant, Howelman, a Hanoverian nobleman, together with the officers of the companies, were all advanced in grade—the names are given in full in the eighth volume of the *Pionier* (1876 to 1877), p. 436.

Of the Pennsylvania Germans who were soldiers in the Revolution, the Hiesters were prominent examples. Four sons of one family were officers: Daniel, the eldest, colonel, John and Gabriel, majors, and William, the youngest, captain; a cousin, Joseph, was in the "Flying Camp," became colonel, later major-general of militia, a member of Congress, and a leader of his party in Berks County down to his death in 1832, in his eightieth year. John and Daniel became major generals of militia, and they, too, were also sent to Congress, one from Pennsylvania and the other from Maryland, where he made his home.

The knowledge of the early Germans, and their share in our history, will no longer be hidden in the records of scattered local periodicals. In the series of *Geschichtsblätter, Bilder u. Mittheilungen aus dem Leben der Deutschen in Amerika, herausgegeben von Carl Schurz,* published in New

York by Steiger, we have the promise of a valuable contribution to our slender stock of available information as to the Germans in the United States. The first volume of this series is a reprint of Kapp's *Die Deutschen im Staate New York während des 18ten Jahrhunderts*, originally published in Leipsic and New York, in 1867. On page 126, there is a list of the officers of the four battalions organized in Schoharie Valley by Germans in 1775 to take part in the war of independence. All four colonels were Germans, viz.: Nicholas Herchheimer, 1st Battalion, Canajoharie; Jacob Kloch, 2nd Battalion, the Pfalz; Friedrich Fischer, 3rd Battalion, Mohawk; Hanjost Herchheimer, 4th Battalion, German Flats.

The Herchheimers were the sons of an early German settler in western New York, who had won distinction by his gallant defense against Indian attacks in the old French war. General Nicholas Herchheimer, who fell in battle in 1777 in defense of the liberties of his country, was honored with the praise of Washington and by a modest monument that perpetuates his services and sacrifice. Born in Germany, one of his soldiers, J. A. Hartmann, survived until 1836, when he died at the age of ninety-two, after an old age of poverty, borne with fortitude. His name is now best remembered in his old home, where he lived at the public expense, as an example of the tardy gratitude of the republic he too had aided to establish. Herchheimer is the type of well-to-do settlers of German descent, Hartmann of the poor emigrant. Still, both did their duty manfully in the struggle for independence and thus set an example freely followed by others, Germans both by birth and descent, who fought for the Union.

Among the leading German soldiers of the Revolutionary War from New York was Hermann von Zedwitz, major of the 1st Regiment; Alfred Schücking sketches his life in *Volume III*, p. 185, of the *Pionier*. The command of Montreal was given to Colonel Rudolph Witzema of the same regiment, an old officer in the Royal Colonial army, who left the Continental Army under a cloud, returned to England, and died there in 1803.

The share of the Germans as officers and soldiers on the patriot side in the war of the Revolution won them the confidence and gratitude of Washington. The Hessians under Riedesel, who surrendered with Burgoyne, were sent to Virginia, where they lived near Jefferson, who thus learned to know them, gave them the use of his library, and enjoyed their music.

The second volume of Schurz's series, *Bilder aus der Deutsch Pennsyl-vanischen Geschichte*, is from the pen of Professor Oswald Seidensticker, whose services in the cause of our local German history have received general acknowledgment for their thoroughness and accuracy. He describes the part taken by the Germans of Pennsylvania in both the Continental Army under Washington and the provincial or state militia. He gives the names of the officers of the German Battalion and their share in the war of independence. In the 2nd, 3rd, 5th, 6th, and 8th Pennsylvania Regiments were many Germans. Colonel Philippe de Haas commanded the 2nd; the lieutenant-colonel of the 3rd was Robert Bunner, who fell at Monmouth in 1778; and Mentges of the 5th and Becker of the 6th were also Germans. Many of these were members of the German Society. Colonel Farmer, first captain of a company of sharpshooters and later commissary-general, was four times president of the German Society after the war.

Reading sent three Hiesters and York many Germans in the regiments that served in the Revolution. Pennsylvania Germans were numerous in Armand's legion, Schott's dragoons, and Van Heer's cavalry brigade. Quakers, Mennonites, Dunkards, and Herrnhüters sacrificed their religious tenets and associations to serve their country. Lutherans and others who had no conscientious scruples against bearing arms were well represented in the field. Foremost among these was General Muhlenberg, born in Montgomery County in 1746, the son of the oldest clergyman of the Lutheran Church in Pennsylvania, who destined all his three sons to follow him in the church, educated at Halle, settled in 1772 in Virginia, as pastor of a German Lutheran congregation in the Shenandoah Valley. He there became a friend of Patrick Henry and Washington. Earnestly supporting the cause of American independence, he became colonel of the 8th Virginia, with Abraham Bowman and Peter Helfenstein as his field-officers. In January 1776, he preached his last sermon, urging on his hearers the duty of patriotic devotion to the cause of the country, and then, throwing aside the clerical gown, showed his military uniform, and instantly over three hundred of his listeners followed his example and joined his regiment. Congress soon made him a brigadier-general, and throughout the war, his zeal, courage, and energy were appreciated by Washington and Lafayette and the other leaders of the Revolution. His part in the final surrender of Cornwallis at Yorktown made him a major-general, and yet so modest was he that when peace returned, his old parishioners would gladly have made him once more their pastor. However, seven years of war had changed the current of this thoughts, and settling in Philadelphia, he became vice-president of the state, under Franklin, and, owing to Franklin's age and infirmities, was practically the head of the government. In 1788 he and his brother worked energetically to secure the adoption of the Constitution of 1789, and under it, he sat in the 1st Congress, as well as in the 2nd and the 6th; always a stout advocate of the Democratic party; he was three times president of the German Society. His descendants, and those of his venerable father, have served the state and the church in many ways and always with honor to their German blood. His statue stands in the Capitol at Washington, as the representative man chosen by Pennsylvania to take a place among the heroes gathered from all parts of the country. His name and his fame are part of the inheritance which the German population of Pennsylvania transmits to future generations to show how thoroughly the German element has done its duty alike in war and peace, and how well it deserves to have its record preserved and published for the information of their descendants and of the country.

GERMAN OFFICERS OF THE REVOLUTIONARY ARMY

GENERAL OFFICERS

DeKalb, John, major general, 1777.
Steuben, F. W. A., major general, 1778.
De Woedtke, Frederick William, brigadier general, 1776.
Muhlenberg, T. P. G., brigadier general, 1777.
Weedon, George, brigadier general, 1777.

Weisenfels, F., lieutenant-colonel, commander 4th New York, 1779.
Ziegler, D., captain 1st Pennsylvania, 1778.

GERMAN BATTALION

Weltener, Ludwick, lieutenant-colonel, 1776.
Burchart, D., major, 1777.
Bunner, J., captain, 1776.
Boyer, P., captain, 1777.
Boetzel, Charles, captain, 1777.
Rice, William, captain, 1778.
Hubley, Bernard, captain, 1778.
Myers, Chr., captain, 1778.
Boyer, Mich., captain, 1778.
Schrauder, Ph., captain, lieutenant, 1778.
Weidman, John, lieutenant, 1777.
Sugart, Martin, lieutenant, 1777.
Gremeth, Jacob, lieutenant, 1778.
Cramer, Jacob, lieutenant, 1778.
Swartz, Godfrey, lieutenant, 1778.
Young, Marcus, lieutenant, 1778.
Morgan, David, lieutenant, 1778.
Weidman, John, ensign, 1777.
Shrupp, Henry, ensign, 1777.
Desenderfer, David, ensign, 1778.
Spech, Henry, ensign, 1778.
Raboldt, Jacob, ensign, 1778.
Glickner, Ch., ensign, 1778.
Prue, William, ensign, 1778.
Hehn, Henry, ensign, 1779.

INDEPENDENT CORPS

Schott, John Paul, captain, 1776.
Selim, Anthony, captain, 1776.

INVALID REGIMENT

Nicola, Lewis, colonel, 1777.
Woelpper, David, captain, 1778.

MARECHAUSEE LIGHT DRAGOONS

Van Heer, Barthol., captain, 1778.
Manaeké, Christ., lieutenant, 1778.
Maitinger, Jac., lieutenant, 1778.
Struebing, Phil., lieutenant, 1778.

ARMAND'S LEGION, CAVALRY

Markle, Chas., captain, 1778.
Schaffner, George, captain, 1778.
Seibert, Henry, lieutenant, 1778.
Schwartz, Godfried, lieutenant, 1778.
Segern, Fred., lieutenant, 1778.
Riedel, Henry, ensign, 1778.

REGULAR ARMY

Bauman, Sebastian, major-commandant Artillery, 1778.
Kalteisen, Michael, captain Artillery, 1794.
Muhlenburg, Henry, lieutenant Artillery, 1794.
Ziegler, David, captain 1st Infantry, 1784.
Strubing, Philip (Van Heer's Corps), captain, brevet, 1784.

Chapter Three

Early Republic

Many of the early settlers of Kentucky were Germans from Virginia and North Carolina, and they held the frontier outposts against the incursions of hostile Indians. Many old Revolutionary soldiers there found homes, and their sons were active in the War of 1812. Frankfort, the state's capital, owes its name to its German founders, for the most part, emigrants from Frankfort-on-the-Main, and its vicinity, who came hither in 1786-87. The first physician was Dr. Louis Marschall, father of Humphrey Marshall noted in Kentucky's civil and military history. Thus, many of the German names were anglicized, some—e.g., Jäger translated into Hunter—completely disguised. Yet, the industry of local historians has shown that Germans made a very large part of Kentucky's early settlement.

Among the soldiers of German descent, a marked and exceptional case is that of General John A. Quitman. He was the son of the pastor of the German Lutheran Church of Schoharie, who was himself born in Iserlohn, Germany, and came to this country in 1795. The father was a strong, determined man, with a high notion of importance, who showed a will of his own not unlike that of the son. The elder Quitman left Schoharie to become pastor of the church in Rhinebeck, where he died in 1832. His son was born there in 1798 and educated by his father's successor. As a young man, he went South, became a distinguished lawyer and member of Congress from his new home in Natchez, Mississippi, took a leading place among the general officers of volunteers in the Mexican War, was prominent in urging on the people of the South the extreme doctrines of states' rights, rejoicing in the name of a fire-eater, and was generally looked on as the intellectual leader of the agitation which finally ended in the Rebellion of 1861. His death, in 1858, saved him from sharing in the devastation his theories had brought over the section which accepted him as their representative.

In the Revolution, there were adherents of Whigs and Tories even in the same family, and this was as true of the Germans as the other nationalities settled in the colonies. In the Rebellion, the minority in either of the two great sections into which the country was divided had little power or influence to stem the tide that finally led to the Union's success. Still, the Germans were found on both sides, for the German's self-reliant, independent character leads him to choose his course and adhere to it despite popular opposition. In Arkansas, Klingelhöffer, son of the founder of a German colony at Little Rock, became an officer of the Confederate Army.

The registers and rolls of the regular army of the United States bear the names of many distinguished soldiers of German birth and descent, and not a few of them brought to the service of their new father-land the training and experience acquired in their native country. In the exhaustive dictionaries of the army by Gardiner and Henry and Hamersly and the invaluable pages of General George W. Cullum's *Record of the Graduates of West Point,* many examples of the German soldier are found in the army of the United States. One example deserves special mention.

John Baptiste de Barth, Baron de Walbach, brigadier-general and colonel commanding 4th Artillery, U.S.A., was the third son of Count Joseph de Barth and Marie Therese de Rohmer. He was born in Munster, Valley of St. Gregory, Upper Rhine, Germany, on the 3rd day of October 1766, and was educated at the military school at Strasbourg. In December 1792, he entered as a cadet the company commanded by Baron de Wald, Regiment of Royal Alsace, Prince Maximillian of Deux Ponts colonel and proprietor, in the service of the King of France. He was promoted and served in the same regiment as an ensign until October 1783, and then until November as gentleman volunteer in the hussars, General Baron de Kellerman commanding. From January 1783 until January 9, 1784, he served in the Regiment of Luzern Hussars, when he received the appointment of sub-lieutenant (cornet), and continued to serve in the successive grades, second lieutenant, first lieutenant, until May 1792, and captain. Declining the commission of captain, he left France to join the armies of the Prince, brother of King Louis XVI. He served in this army as a gentleman volunteer, on horseback, at his own expense, under Colonel Count de Pestalozzi, his former colonel of the Luzern Hussars. With this corps, he made the campaign in Champagne, in 1792, in advance of the Prussian army, until it was disbanded in Maastricht. He then left Liege, passed through the French lines to Treves, and brought back his sister, Mme. Blondeau, and placed her, with their three children, under the care of her husband, lieutenant-colonel, formerly major, of artillery, who had served in the army of Rochambeau in America. He then went to Germany, took part in the attack on Frankfort, January 6, 1793, and later joined the Sixty-second Company, 1st Battalion of the Austrian Chasseurs of Condé, serving, during the campaign of 1793, in attacks on the French lines at Germersheim, Yorkheim, Langenkardet, and Weissembourg, where the Austrians captured one hundred and fifty-five pieces of cannon; the losses in both armies being estimated at twenty-two thousand men. He then accepted a captaincy from the Prince de Rohan and covered the retreat of the Duke of York's unfortunate army northward to Holland and Germany. Finally, he embarked with his regiment, the Hussars of Rohan, for the British West Indies, on the promise of the British Government that they should always serve on horseback and that at the end of four years, they were being returned to their homes. In 1798, being then the third officer of the regiment, which had been reduced by yellow fever from twelve hundred to one hundred and thirty, he obtained leave for six months to visit his father, who had come to America at the outbreak of the French Revolution. With twenty-four other noblemen, he had agreed to buy forty thousand acres of land on the Scioto River, Ohio, paying half the purchase-money to Joel Barlow and William Playfair, agents in Paris of Colonel William Duer, accredited by a letter from Thomas Jefferson. Count de Barth sailed with three hundred emigrants, landed in Alexandria, Virginia, in March 1790, and then proceeded to Marietta, Ohio, where he found that Duer had become bankrupt. He returned to Philadelphia, purchased a country-seat—Springettsbury Manor, Bush Hill, a mansion with sixty acres—but he died there September 24, 1793. He was buried in St. Mary's Roman Catholic Church in Philadelphia.

Bush Hill was occupied as a hospital during the yellow fever, and as there was no one authorized to make the last payment, it was sold by the sheriff and passed from the family. In 1798 Colonel, then Major, Walbach, on his arrival, retained Messrs. William Rawle, Jared Ingersoll, and James Heatly, but owing to the loss of documents, could obtain no redress. Major Walbach then resigned his commission as major in the Hussars of Rohan and became an adopted citizen of the United States. In the autumn of 1798, he entered the United States Army on the invitation of Washington, Hamilton, and McHenry, as a second lieutenant of cavalry, and was appointed adjutant of a cavalry regiment, holding that post until the corps was disbanded in June 1799. He then was employed in the office of the Adjutant-General of the United States, General William North, who had been an aid to General Steuben. In December 1799, he was employed to assist General Charles C. Pinckney in preparing regulations for the cavalry and assisting General Hamilton in preparing regulations for the artillery. Afterward, he was ordered to report to General Washington to take charge of a detachment of dragoons. He was appointed, in 1801, a first lieutenant in the 1st Regiment of Artillery and Engineers, and in 1802 aid to General Wilkinson; in 1804, adjutant of artillery and military agent at Fort Constitution, New Hampshire; in 1806, captain of the artillery; in 1812, assistant deputy quartermaster; in 1813, assistant adjutant-general with the rank of major, and assistant adjutant-general with the rank of colonel, and brevet major; for gallant conduct at the Battle of Chrystler's Fields; in 1815, major of artillery and brevet lieutenant-colonel; in 1830, brevet colonel for ten years' further service, and lieutenant-colonel in the 1st Regiment of Artillery; in

1842, colonel of the 4th Regiment of Artillery, and made commander at Fortress Monroe and brevet brigadier-general; and in 1851 he was assigned to the command of the Department of the East. He died in Baltimore, Maryland, on June 10, 1857, of disease contracted in the War of 1812. At the time of his death, General Scott, lieutenant-general commanding, issued a highly commendatory order reciting his long military career, his distinguished services, and his unwavering integrity, truth, and honor, strict attention to duty, and zeal for the service, tempering the administration of an exact discipline by the most elevated courtesies. General George W. Cullum, in his *Campaigns and Engineers of the War of 1812-15*, at page 168, credits him with saving the artillery at Chrystler's Fields in 1813. His grandson, John de Barth Walbach Gardiner, was an assistant surgeon in the United States Army. His son, L. de B. Walbach, who died in 1853, was a West Point graduate and a captain of ordnance. Another son died an officer of the United States navy.

Old officers of the regular army well remember general Walbach as a fine soldierly character, full of zeal and pride in his profession, and a man of many manly virtues and attractive qualities. His brother was a Roman Catholic priest in Baltimore, and in their old age, these two men, living together, were typical examples of the professions of war and peace.*

Among the early graduates of West Point, a notable example of how Germany has supplied our army with officers is the case of Julius F. Heileman, son of the surgeon of Riedesel's German Brigade in Burgoyne's army; he was appointed a cadet in 1803, and rose to be major of the 2nd Artillery, when he fell in Florida, in 1836.

---

* The battle of Leipsic, the turning-point of the uprising of Germany against Napoleon, was celebrated in Philadelphia by German citizens, with toasts in honor of the Emperor of Russia, the burning of Moscow, Blücher, the German Princes, and the Patriots of South America.

Conrad Weiser.

General Edward Braddock

Early American Indian War

Colonel Henry Bouquet

Frederik the Great, King of Prussia

General Baron von Steuben

General Baron deKalb

Lewis Wetzel killing three Indians

The Death of General Montgomery at Quebec

General Herkimer at Oriskany

General Peter Muhlenberg

Colonel Josiah Harmar

General George Weedon

Daniel Hiester

William Hiester

Joseph Hiester

Colonel Philippe de Haas

John A. Quitman

General John de Barth Walbach

General Herman Haupt

General Samuel P. Heintzelman

Francis Lieber

General August V Kautz

Brevet Lieutenant Colonel Alfred Mordecai

General George Armstrong Custer

Lieutenant John Trout Greble

General Godfrey Weitzel

Colonel Alexander von Schrader   General Henry A. Hambright

Gustav Schleicher

General Galusha Pennypacker

General John F Hartranft

General Isaac Jones Wistar

Colonel Langhorne Wistar

Colonel William Rotch Wistar

Brevet Brigadier General J. William
Hofmann

Colonel John A. Koltes

General Samuel K Zook

Brevet Brigadier General Louis Wagner

Captain Charles Godfrey Freudenberg

Cartoonist Thomas H Nast

Nast cartoon

Carl Schurz

General Adolph von Steinwehr

Colonel Leopold von Gilsa

Colonel Hugo Wangelin

Governor Gustav Körner

Colonel Friedrich Hecker

Colonel Emile Frey, Swiss Minister to the USA

General Peter J Osterhaus

Colonel Franz Hassendeubel

General Franz Sigel

Major General Franz Sigel

General August Willich

Colonel Charles E. Salomon

Andrew Dickson White

Chapter Four

Civil War

George Nauman was a graduate of West Point in 1823, who rose by slow but good service and died as lieutenant-colonel of the 1st Artillery in Philadelphia in 1863. He was born in Pennsylvania sixty years before.

General Ammen, who was distinguished during the Rebellion, was a native of Virginia, a graduate of West Point in 1831, had resigned to engage in teaching and engineering, and when the war broke out, re-entered the service as colonel of the 24th Ohio; as a brigadier-general, he served with great bravery in the West.

Edmund Schriver and Alexander Shiras were graduates of 1833, and both were born in Pennsylvania. Their services in the Rebellion were highly appreciated.

Herman Haupt, a graduate of 1835, was born in Philadelphia and, besides his services in the field, has been a pioneer in the great business of railroad building across the continent. His son graduated in 1867.

Luther, Roland, and Hagner, all the class of 1836, bore good Pennsylvania German names.

The Muhlenbergs have had a representative, and often more than one, in the regular army since the time of the early Pennsylvania soldier down to our day, and all have done honor to a name that is looked on as one fittingly chosen as the type of the Pennsylvania soldier and statesman. The Muhlenbergs, six at least, fill an honored place on the registers of the regular army, in which they have a right by descent from patriot ancestors of the Revolution.

General S. P. Heintzelman, a veteran of the regular army, was born in Lancaster County in 1805. His grandfather, a native of Augsburg, was the first white settler in Manheim, where his grandson was educated until he went to West Point in 1826. He was promoted and brevetted for his gallantry in the Mexican War, and at the outbreak of the Rebellion, became colonel of the 17th United States Infantry. At Bull Run, he was wounded; on the Peninsula, he commanded a corps, and throughout the war, he was always on duty.

Francis Lieber was born in Berlin in 1800; he grew up amid the earnest aspirations of Germany for freedom from the French yoke, and at the age of fifteen, following the example of his elder brothers, and with the approval of his parents, enlisted in the Colberg Regiment under Blücher. He began his short experience of war at Ligny, was wounded, and returned after the Waterloo campaign to resume his work as a school-boy. With the other young Turners, he followed Jahn in his plan for political and physical regeneration, and with his leader, he was imprisoned for excess of patriotism. His four months confinement was not in itself a great hardship, but it carried with it a prohibition to study in any Prussian university, and this implied his exclusion from public employment. He studied at Jena, Halle, and Dresden, and then at twenty-one took part in the Greek struggle, with very unsatisfactory results.

Then, encouraged by Niebuhr, in whose family he had been employed in Rome, he returned to Berlin, only to be again imprisoned. Enforced idleness ensued. He composed a volume of poems of the merriest kind; after trying in vain to secure a stable position, he freed himself from the uncomfortable results of his early patriotism by coming to America, where he arrived in 1827. He established a swimming school in Boston after the model of those of Germany but soon undertook a very great work—the preparation of the *Encyclopædia Americana*, based on Brockhaus's *Conversations Lexicon*, published in Philadelphia, which then became the scene of his active literary labors. He prepared an elaborate scheme for the management of Girard College and began his independent authorship. He went to the University of South Carolina, in 1835, as a Professor of History and Political Economy. There he wrote and taught until 1857 when he gladly left the South.

When the Rebellion broke out, he was quietly settled at Columbia College in New York. One of his sons went into the Confederate service, another with the Illinois troops into the Union army, and a third got a commission in the regular army. He began his work as a legal advisor to the government on military and international law questions by preparing a code of instructions for the government of armies of the United States in the field. From that time on, he was in constant employment in that direction, putting his vast store of learning at the disposition of the authorities on every fitting occasion. He maintained a close correspondence with the leading German professors Bluntschli, Mohl, Holtzendorff, and did much to secure in Germany a proper appreciation of the great work done for the world by securing the perpetuation of the American Union, and later to make America alive to the merits of the great struggle with France which secured German unity. His busy life ended in 1872. His best epitaph was his favorite motto, "Patria Cara, Carior Libertas, Veritas Carissima," for Country, Liberty, and Truth were the great aims in all he wrote and spoke and thought. His services were of a kind not often within the reach and range of a single life, and his memory deserves to be honored and kept green in both his native and his adopted country. He was well represented in the Union cause by his two sons, Hamilton, who served in the Ninety-second Illinois and died in 1876, an officer of the regular army, and Guido, still in the regular service, though whom his name is perpetuated in the army register, while the death of another son on the Confederate side was another sacrifice to the cause of the Union.

His *Instructions for Armies in the Field, General Order No. 100*, published by the Government of the United States, April 24, 1863, were the first codification of international articles of war and marked an epoch in the history of international law and of civilization. His other contributions to military and to international law, published at various times during the Civil War, together with his other miscellaneous writings on political science, have been reprinted in the two volumes of his works issued by J. B. Lippincott & Co., in 1881, and these, with his memoirs and the tributes paid him by President Gilman and Judge Thayer, are his best monument. A memoir by T. S. Perry well deserves attention, and the German translation, edited by Holtzendorff, shows Lieber's popularity in Germany.

General August V. Kautz was born in Baden in 1828 and came as a lad to this country, where his family settled in Ohio. At the outbreak of the Mexican War, he enlisted in the 1st Ohio Regiment and was rewarded for his services by being appointed a lieutenant in the regular army. He was a captain of the cavalry at the outbreak of the Rebellion, commanded his regiment, the 6th Cavalry, under McClellan, in the operations before Richmond, was appointed colonel of the 2nd Ohio Cavalry and chief of cavalry of the 23rd Corps, and brevetted major-general in both the volunteer and regular service. He became lieutenant-colonel of the 15th Infantry after the war, is now colonel of the 8th Infantry, and is the author of some excellent works on various military science subjects.

Brevet Lieutenant-Colonel Alfred Mordecai, of the Ordnance Department of the United States Army, is a graduate of West Point of June 1861 and is now major of his corps. His scientific services have been recognized both in and out of the army. He is the son of a distinguished officer of the regular army, Major A. Mordecai, of the class of 1823, whose military record was a very brilliant one; his name is familiar as the author, with General McClellan and General Delafield, of an admirable report of their visit to Europe and the Crimea during the Russian war of 1854. His grandfather was a German. Father and son have both contributed to the science of their branch of the military profession, ordnance. The elder, Major Mordecai, gave the first impulse to Professor Henry's application of electricity to ballistics—the art of measuring the velocity of projectiles, now become a matter of everyday use in all arsenals throughout the world.

General George A. Custer, one of the most picturesque characters of the war and an exceptional soldier in his Indian campaigns, was the great-grandson of an officer of the Hessian soldiers sent here to serve in the British army during the Revolution. After Burgoyne's surrender, his ancestor, paroled in 1778, settled in Pennsylvania, married there, changed his German name, Küster, to one easier to pronounce in English, and moved to Maryland, where the father of General Custer was born in 1806. His famous son was born in Ohio in 1839, as a boy taught school in his native village, Hopedale, until 1857, when he was appointed a cadet at West Point. Graduating there in June 1861, he was assigned to the 2nd Cavalry, served with distinction, was made a captain on the staff of General McClellan, served with General Kearney and General Pleasanton, was appointed a brigadier-general for his gallantry at the Battle of Aldie, and commanded, successively, a brigade and a division of cavalry, which he led with distinguished bravery. He was promoted to be a major-general of volunteers, a brevet major-general of the United States Army, and lieutenant-colonel of the 7th Cavalry, served under General Hancock in a series of campaigns against the Indians, and finally fell in battle with the Sioux. He was the author of many capital contributions to the periodical literature after the Civil War, and his memory is preserved in his wife's charming little book, *Military Life on the Frontiers*, and in the *Life of General Custer*, by F. Whittaker, published shortly after his heroic death in June 1876.

Lieutenant John T. Greble of the 2nd Artillery, a graduate of West Point class of 1854, is well remembered as the first officer of the regular army to fall in the war of the Rebellion. Born in Philadelphia in 1834, he was killed in action, at Big Bethel, Virginia, on the 10th of June, 1861. He was one of the most popular officers in the service, distinguished alike for gallantry and attainments. He, too, was of German descent, and the traditions of the family were all patriotic. His great-grandfather, Andrew Greble, a native of Saxe-Gotha, came to this country in 1742, settled permanently in Philadelphia, and enlisted warmly in the cause of the War of Independence. He and his four sons joined the American army and fought at the battles of Princeton and Monmouth. Two of his ancestors on his mother's side, good Welsh Quakers, were in the Continental Army. A graduate of the Philadelphia High School, he showed at West

Point and in the army a love of study, which, with his amiable manners and soldierly conduct, secured him the friendship of all with whom he was brought in contact. After serving in Florida, he was appointed to the corps of instructors at West Point and was on duty at Fortress Monroe when the Civil War broke out. His untimely death was due to his deliberate purpose to sacrifice his life to save the lives of the large body of soldiers imperiled by an overwhelming force. His heroism had its reward in the gratitude with which his memory is cherished both in the army and by the people. His son, Lieutenant Edwin St. John Greble, a graduate of 1881, is now serving with the 2nd United States Artillery.

William Heine was born in 1827, died in Dresden, his native city, in October 1885. He learned landscape and architectural painting in Paris and was employed as a painter at the Dresden Court Theatre, but, after the revolution of 1848 in Saxony, came to the United States in 1851; he traveled in Central America, which he described in *Wanderbilder aus Centralamerika*, Leipzig, 1853. He subsequently joined Perry's expedition to Japan, and, in 1860, the Prussian expedition to the same country, describing it in his *Japan, Beiträge zur Kentniss des Landes u.s. Bewohner*, Dresden, 1870. After the outbreak of the American Civil War, he entered the Union army as captain of engineers; advanced to the rank of brigadier, March 1865; was afterward employed in the United States consular service and returned to his native land in 1871.

The Germans served in large numbers in cavalry and artillery companies of volunteers in the Mexican War, notably from Texas and Missouri. Many of them gained distinction in this service. Kentucky had its infantry regiment and its cavalry company of Germans in the Mexican War and many Germans in its loyal regiments during the Rebellion, notably Companies E and G of the 4th Cavalry and Barth's company of the 28th Kentucky Volunteers. Among the Germans whose services in Texas ought not to be forgotten is the once familiar name of William Langenheim. Of his associates, Gustavus Schleicher in Texas and J. A. Wagener in South Carolina served in the Confederate army. New Orleans and Louisiana had two representative Germans—Christian Roselius and Michael Hahn, among their leading Union men.

General Godfrey Weitzel was born in Germany in 1835 and came with his parents to this country. He was appointed a cadet at West Point in his seventeenth year, and in 1855 graduated as a lieutenant of engineers. He served with Butler and Banks in the South and led a division under Grant in the final conquest of Richmond. After the war, he was constantly employed in his profession until his untimely death in Philadelphia, March 19, 1884.

Colonel Alexander von Schrader, born in Germany, a soldier by training, was lieutenant-colonel of the Seventy-fourth Ohio, and became a major in the 39th Infantry of the regular army, dying in service August 6, 1867. He had been reduced to the direst poverty before the war, but when the occasion came, his distinguished gallantry and efficient military training stood him in good stead.

Henry A. Hambright, retired as major 19th United States Infantry, brevet colonel United States Army, brevet brigadier-general United States volunteers, was born in Lancaster, Pennsylvania, on March 24, 1819. His father, Frederick, a major-general of militia, and his uncle, George, a colonel, both served in the War of 1812. Colonel Hambright served in the Mexican War, in the War of the Rebellion as an officer of the 2nd Pennsylvania Volunteers, in the 1st Pennsylvania (three months) Volunteers, and as colonel of the Seventy-ninth Pennsylvania; while still in the three months' service he was commissioned captain of the 11th United States Infantry, and served with distinguished gallantry through the war, and with great fidelity until he was retired for a disability incurred in the line of duty.

A study of the register of officers of the regular army from 1779 shows a large proportion of Germans—beginning with Kalb and Steuben, in the German Battalion of Pennsylvania and Maryland, the artillery and engineer and other staff corps engaged in the wars of 1812 and 1846. During the Rebellion, many old soldiers of German birth were rewarded by commissions, and not a few distinguished German volunteers were also appointed in the regular army—among them Blücher, Von Hermann, Luettwitz, Michalowski, Von Schirach.

There were two million six hundred and ninety thousand men engaged in the army and navy during the Rebellion, besides seventy-two thousand emergency men called out for short periods of service. The Count of Paris, in his exhaustive history of the war, says that of the volunteers who enlisted during the first year, only one-tenth were foreigners; of the remainder, two-thirds were born on American soil, and less than one-fourth were naturalized Europeans. In 1864, when conscription was partially resorted to, eighty percent were natives. This army, more than two-thirds natives and less than one-third foreigners, was raised out of a population of nineteen million. Far more than one-third of the effective male population was of European birth, yet there was less than that proportion in the army ranks.

At the time of the Battle of Bull Run, the Confederacy had about two hundred thousand men under arms. When the North called for five hundred thousand men, the South called for four hundred thousand. In 1862 the South had about one hundred and eighty thousand men in the field; in April of that year, the Confederate Congress ordered, not a draft as in the past, but a levy en masse of all white males between eighteen and thirty-five, residing within the Confederacy, for three years or the war, divided into sixteen classes. Based on a population of five million whites, this should have produced eight hundred thousand men—it did give between four and five hundred thousand effective men. In September 1862, the limit of age was extended to forty-five, and the other limit was made to include all who had completed their seventeenth year since April.

In the Confederate army, there were many Germans, and much of the literature of the war on the part of the South is made up of the records of those who served on that side—notable among them Heros von Borcke, and he speaks in his Munchausen-like book of finding among the riflemen an old Prussian soldier from Texas—of meeting at Lee's headquarters Captain Scheibert, of the Prussian engineers, detailed as an observer, but taking an active part as a combatant—and the author of a book, *Sieben Monate in den Rebellen Staaten*, published in Stettin in

1868, characterized by its strong Southern tone.* Then there is the book of another German soldier of fortune, B. Estvan, whose *Kriegsbilder aus Amerika* appeared in Leipsic in 1864, as it had already been published in England and New York in English in 1863. Fritz Annecke, a soldier in the West, published a work on *Der zweite Freiheitskrieg,* in Frankfort in1861—H. Blankenburg another coming down to the Presidential election in 1868 (Leipsic, 1869); August Conrad *Schatten und Lichtbilder aus dem amerikanischen Leben wahrend des Secessionskrieges* (Hannover, 1879); Rüstow, a recognized authority on war, a history of the war, from a purely military point of view. Mangold wrote *Der Feldzug in Neu Virginien in August 1862* (Hannover, 1881), which has received high praise—Constantin Sander, a history of the war, first down to 1862, and then a later and more complete volume, the former published in Frankfort in 1863, the second in 1865. *Von Achten der Letzte* is a German novel on the Southern side published in Wiesbaden in 1871. Much that is of interest on the subject is to be found in the volume, *In der neuen*

---

* In McClellan's admirable life of General J. E. B. Stuart, there is a paper signed by that distinguished officer under date of June 17, 1862, in which he says,—

"M. Heros von Borcke, a Prussian cavalry officer, has shown himself a thorough soldier and a splendid officer. I hope the [War] Department will confer as high a commission as possible on this deserving man, who has cast in his lot with us in this trying hour." (p. 69.)

At page 307, we find that on the 19th of August, 1863, Major Heros von Borcke, an officer of the Prussian army, who was serving on General Stuart's staff, received a severe wound, which disabled him from further service. (p. 307.)

In the *Southern Bivouac Magazine,* for February, 1886, published a Louisville, Kentucky, it is mentioned at page 515 that the distinguished Colonel Von Borcke, Stuart's chief-of-staff, lately revisited Fauquier County, Virginia, staying near Upperville, on the northern border; his once robust constitution much affected by the ball he still carries in his right lung, received when he was wounded in 1863; but his jovial, impulsive, warm-hearted nature has not forsaken him. Colonel Von Borcke served on the staff of Prince Frederic Charles, in the war of 1866, but his old wounds forced him to retire.

Captain Scheibert's interest in the Southern cause did not end with the war; on returning to Germany, where he became major in the Prussian Engineers, he corresponded with the editor of the Southern Historical Society's Papers. In vol. v., p. 90, his letter on Gettysburg, dated Stuttgart, November 21, 1879, is printed, and in vol. iv., p. 88, there is a notice by Colonel Venables, C.S.A., of a translation of Scheibert's book into French, by Captain Bonnecque, of the French Engineers. In 1883, Major Scheibert published a German translation of Allan's *History of the Valley Campaign*; and in a letter of October 13, 1881, dated at Hirshberg, Silesia, Prussia, he says he has translated and printed in German, Early's *Gettysburg,* Stuart's and Lee's *Reports,* Hubbard's *Chancellorsville,* Patton's *Jackson,* McClellan's *Jeb Stuart,* Stuart's *Gettysburg,* and biographies of Lee, Jackson, Stuart, and Mosby. His B*urgerkrieg in den Vereinigten Staaten* has been translated into French and Spanish.

Heimath, Geschichtliche Mittheilungen über die Deutschen Einwanderer in allen Theilen der Union, herausgegeben von Anton Eickhoff, Ausgabe, New York, Steiger, 1885, 8vo, pp. 398.

Of translations and newspaper magazine articles in German, the number is almost endless. Many Southern citizens living abroad tried to reach the German public by arguments and appeals. Still, the fact remains that the great mass of the German people was from first to last unshaken in their faith in the Union's success. They profited largely by the faith, which led them to make investments in American bonds and securities at a time of general doubt.

In North Carolina, there were many Germans and the descendants of the early German settlers in the Confederate service. In Wilmington, North Carolina, at the commencement of the war, a company was raised under the name of the German Volunteers, afterward Company A, 18th Regiment North Carolina troops. The officers were C. Cornehlsen, Captain; H. Vollers, 1st Lieutenant; G. H. W. Runge, 2nd Lieutenant; E. Schulken, 3rd Lieutenant. There were seventy-five men rank and file, all Germans, in this organization, while in other branches of the service, artillery and cavalry, and the Confederate States navy, there were Germans—so that North Carolina had a fair share of them in its volunteers.

South Carolina was not without its German soldiers. Indeed, as early as 1670, the first German that set foot in Carolina, John Lederer, made a tour of exploration under the direction of Governor William Berkeley, of Virginia; he was a man of learning; his journal was written in Latin, and the translator, Sir William Talbot, Governor of Maryland, speaks highly of his literary attainments. The account of this journey was published and circulated and doubtless had its effect in the settling of Carolina, for it is certain that in 1680 German immigration had fairly set in. In 1764 six hundred Palatines arrived in South Carolina. In 1766 the German Friendly Society was founded in Charleston, and as early as 1686, the German Lutherans were included among the leading elements of the population. Between 1730 and 1750, a great addition was made from Switzerland and Germany. The dreadful war that scourged the peaceful inhabitants for so many years drove thousands to America, and of these, many came to Carolina. Of course, in the Confederacy, and especially in its army from South Carolina and in defense of Charleston, there were many Germans; thus, in the force that took possession of Fort Moultrie in April 1861, there was the German Artillery, Captain C. Nohrden; and among the troops furnished by the city of Charleston to the Southern army, in the roster printed in Courtenay's *History of Charleston*, are the following German organizations, viz.:

- 4th Brigade South Carolina Militia: German Riflemen, Captain J. Small; Palmetto Riflemen, Captain A. Melchers.
- 17th Infantry, German Fusileers, Captain S. Lord, Jr.
- 1st Regiment of Artillery, Major John A. Wagener (a veteran of the war with Mexico, a member of Company F, the Charleston company of the South Carolina Regiment).
- German Artillery, Company A, Captain C. Nohrden; German Artillery, Company B, Captain H. Harms.
- Cavalry, German Hussars, Captain Theodore Cordes.
- Marion Rifles, a volunteer corps of the fire department, Captain C. B. Sigwald.

At the commencement of the War of the Rebellion, the Germans of Charleston, South Carolina, took an active share in the war. They considered that the North assailed their homes, and they volunteered freely for the war, furnishing about four hundred men. The German Artillery, Companies A and B, were militia organizations under Major John A. Wagener's command. These two companies served from the outset until the war ended. The two companies were under the respective command of Captains A. Nohrden and H. Harms. After the Battle of Hilton Head, November 7, 1861, Major Wagener took command of Charleston's Home Guards. Company A's commander was Captain D. Werner; of Company B, Captain Franz Melchers, who served during the rest of the war. After the war, the command was reorganized as one company under Captain F. W. Wagener, who had served during the war after Captain Wagener's resignation. The German Hussars, also a militia company, volunteered for the war under Captain Theodore Cordes; Captain Fremder took command on his death. After his death, Captain Hanke Wohlken served during the war. The German Volunteers were a company of young men under Captain W. K. Bachman; they volunteered for and served throughout the war. All of them declared their allegiance to the home they had chosen voluntarily and shared the fate of the people who had received them kindly, while they hardly bothered their heads about the cause of the war. They were merchants, clerks, artisans, etc., and many of them have passed away during or since the war. Captain F. Melchers still survives— for forty years, a resident of Charleston. For thirty-three years, he was the *Deutsche Zeitung* publisher, except during the four years of the war, when he served as a lieutenant and captain and as lieutenant-colonel on the staff of General Wade Hampton. Captain F. W. Wagener and Captain Hanke Wohlken are merchants; Captain W. R. Bachman, a lawyer, and Professor C. H. Bergmann, of the German School, was a volunteer and orderly sergeant in Bachman's company during the war. The survivors are about to erect a monument to their fallen comrades, and the Germans of Charleston have contributed a handsome sum for the purpose.

The Charleston companies in the armies of the Confederate States for the war (1861-1865) included in Courtenay's roster:

- Three companies of German artillery.
- Light Battery B,[*] Hampton Legion, Captain W. K. Bachman.
- Light Battery A, Captain F. W. Wagener.
- Light Battery B, Captain F. Melchers.
- Marion Rifles, Company A, 24th Regiment South Carolina Volunteers, Captain C. B. Sigwald.
- German Hussars, Troop G, 3rd Regiment South Carolina Cavalry, Captain Theodore Cordes.

In Texas, many Germans served in the Confederate army. In Walker's Texas Division, the 3rd Texas Volunteer Infantry Regiment had

---

[*] This company, called the German Volunteers, was raised by the German citizens of Charleston, mustered into service for the war as an infantry company, and subsequently transferred to the light artillery.

Company B, Captain Biesenbuch, Lieutenants Koening and Uhl; Company F, Captain Rosenheimer, Lieutenants Ztuni and Hafner; Company G, Captain Sherhagen; Company K, Captain Bosi, Lieutenants Sarasin and Schleuning. In the 16th Texas, Colonel Flournoy, Company E, Captain G. T. Marold, Lieutenants Klaedon, Hanke and Groff; Company H, of the 17th, Captain Sabath, Lieutenant Kollmauer, were all Germans.

In the 1st Virginia Infantry, Company K had Lieutenants C. Bauman, B. Bergmeier, and A. Bitzel (see its history by Charles Loehr).

The Louisiana militia organizations at the outset of the Rebellion included the New Orleans Jägers, Captain Peters, Lieutenants Fassbinder and Huth; the Sharpshooters, Captain Christern; the Fusileers, Captain Sievers, Lieutenants Gerdes and Walbrack; the LaFayette Guards, Captain Koenig, Lieutenants Hollenback and Fridebach; the Jefferson Guards, Captain Wollrath, Lieutenant Lehman; Reichard's Battalion; Turner Guards, Captain Bahncke, Lieutenants Von Armlinsen, Eicholz, Schneider; Steuben Guards, Captain Burger, Lieutenants Kehrwald, Rosenbaum, Hausner; Reichard Rifles, Captain Reitmeyer, Lieutenants Weise, De Petz, Muller; Louisiana Volunteers, Captain Ruhl, Lieutenants Von Zincken, Darrel; Black Jägers, Captain Robenhorst; Florence Guards, Captain Brummenstadt, Lieutenants Lachenmeyer, Wassernagel, Warburg. Bachman's was one of the batteries of the Washington Artillery of New Orleans, and Colonel Waggaman commanded the 10th Louisiana.

In Georgia, among the troops engaged in defense of Fort Pulaski were the German Volunteers, Captain John H. Stegin, one of the companies of the 1st Volunteer Regiment of Georgia.

The register of Confederate States army contains the following German names: Colonels J. T. Holtzclaw, 18th Alabama, Brigadier-General; A. H. Helvenstein, 16th Alabama; E. Waggaman, 10th Louisiana; L. C. Gause, 32nd Arkansas; Major W. O. Yager, 3rd Texas Cavalry; Captain R. M. Gans, 4th Texas Cavalry; Colonel J. N. Adenbousch, 2nd Virginia Infantry; Colonel J. N. Waul, 10th Texas, Brigadier-General; Captain F. C. Schulz, Chestnut Artillery, South Carolina; Captain C. R. Hanleiter, Jr., Thompson's Artillery, Georgia; J. A. Englehard, Major and Assistant

Adjutant-General, Pender's Light Division, 3rd Corps; R. W. Memminger, Assistant Adjutant-General and Chief of Staff, Department of Mississippi and East Louisiana.

Gustav Schleicher was the first German in Congress who won a reputation as a representative of the Germans of the United States. Born in Darmstadt in 1823, he studied at Giessen, became a successful civil engineer, emigrated to Texas in 1847, established himself finally in San Antonio, served, successively, in both branches of the Texas Legislature, was lieutenant-colonel and colonel of the Texas Rangers in the Confederate army, and was elected to the United States Congress in 1874 as a German Democrat. He showed marked ability, thorough training, and conscientious study. Re-elected twice to Congress, his premature death in 1879 cut short a career that gave promise of honor to himself and usefulness to his adopted country.

The statistics of the nativity of the states› population at the time of the Rebellion are not to be absolutely ascertained. I find in *Freiheit u. Sklaverei unter dem Sternenbanner, oder Land u. Leute in Amerika,* by Theodore Griesinger, Stuttgart, 1862, the statement that in Pennsylvania there were then over a million of German birth and descent; in New York, 800,000; in Ohio, 600,000; in New Jersey, 125,000; in New England, 30,000; while there were in the Southern States, in Virginia, 250,000; in Maryland, 125,000; in Missouri, over 100,000; in Louisiana, 50,000; in Texas, 30,000; in Tennessee, 50,000; in North Carolina and Kentucky, 70,000; in Delaware, 25,000; in South Carolina, 20,000; in the cotton states—Georgia, Alabama, Mississippi, and Arkansas, 10,000; in Florida, 5000. There is no estimate of the number in the Northwest, that vast region from which came the volunteers of Illinois, Indiana, Michigan, Wisconsin, and Iowa. Of course, the Germans of Missouri supplied large numbers of soldiers, some of them of great distinction. Many Germans from other States went to Missouri, which was almost the first seat of active operations. Fremont and Sigel and Asboth attracted Germans from all quarters, just as in the East, German regiments asked to join Blenker's brigade until it became a division. Others were ready to swell the division to a corps. Indeed, it was from Blenker's demand to lead it that McClellan was obliged to administer a reproof which led finally to his resignation from active service.

The only attempt at an official analysis of the nativity of the soldiers of the Union army is that found in a volume of medical statistics published in a final report of the Provost-Marshal General, General James B. Fry, U.S.A., in which it is stated that out of 343,764 drafted men there were from Württemberg, 1; Austria, 67; Prussia, 754; Bavaria, 35; Saxony, 15; Germany, 35,935; Switzerland, 1158; total, 37,965; but in another place it is said that there were of German birth 54,944 soldiers drafted in the service. In the same report, it is said that thirty percent of the American army were of foreign birth during the Mexican War and that this proportion held good of the volunteers during the Rebellion, but that in times of peace, the proportions were reversed, seventy percent of the recruits being of foreign birth. It is also stated that twenty-four nationalities were represented in the United States Army. Out of a total of a million two hundred and fifty thousand men actually in the war, there were seventy-five thousand Germans. This is certainly very far short of the actual number and is by no means borne out as accurate even by the estimates made by the very competent authority of the statistician employed by the United States Sanitary Commission, Dr. B. A. Gould, whose tables are based upon very careful mathematical data, and come as near the truth as can be expected in the absence of absolute returns.

The United States Sanitary Commission, in addition to its other good work, has published *Investigations in the Statistics of American Soldiers*, by B. A. Gould (New York, 1869), of which one chapter is devoted to the nativity of the United States Volunteers (chap. ii., pp. 15-26). It gives a suggestive list of the arrivals of aliens in the United States, as follows:

1860	153,640
1861	112,705
1862	114,475
1863	199,811
1864	221,535

Thirty in every hundred alien passengers before 1861, and thirty-three in each hundred during the war, were males of military age, and the total for the years of the war may be placed at two hundred and twenty-nine thousand five hundred and thirty-two.

It was not until the war had been waged for some time that the place of birth was systematically required on the enlistment rolls; the actual records are therefore very imperfect, and as many men enlisted at different times for different periods—in one instance, five times—even regimental statistics are misleading. It was not until the organization of the provost marshal general's office that nativity was made an essential element of each soldier's history. Out of the two and a half million men in the army, the nativities of about one million two hundred thousand have been collected for Dr. Gould's work from the records at the national and State capitals, of about two hundred and ninety-three thousand from regimental officers. In Missouri, it was estimated that there were ten thousand re-enlistments among the German population, but making due allowance for these, the Sanitary Commission gives the following table of Germans, volunteers in the different regiments from the states, and in the parallel column that of the proportion the Germans would have borne to the native and other nationalities in the populations of each state, and I have added the German population from the census of 1860 in another column:

From	Number of German Soldiers	Proportions to whole Population	Total German Population. Census of 1860.
Maine	244	34	2,601
New Hampshire	952	35	412
Vermont	86	19	219
Massachusetts	1,876	860	9,961
Rhode Island and Connecticut	2,919	825{R. I. Conn.	845 8,525
New York	36,680	22,591	256,252
New Jersey	7,387	3,097	33,772
Pennsylvania	17,208	13,173	138,244
Delaware	621	139	1,263
Maryland	3,107	2,373	43,884
District of Columbia	746	643	3,254
West Virginia	869	194 (Va.)	10,512
Kentucky	1,943	1,276	27,227
Ohio	20,102	18,984	168,210
Indiana	7,190	7,793	66,705
Illinois	18,140	16,647	130,804
Michigan	3,534	3,793	38,787
Wisconsin	15,709	12,729	123,879
Minnesota	2,715	2,172	18,400
Iowa	2,850	3,239	38,555
Missouri	30,899	7,105	88,487
Kansas	1,090	692	4,318
A grand total of	187,858	128,102	1,118,402

And as against this, there were

	Population to Population.	Volunteers
British Americans	22,695	53,532
English	38,250	45,508
Irish	139,052	144,221
Other foreigners	39,455	48,410
Foreigners not otherwise designated	278	26,445

Adding to these native Americans, 1,523,267 makes a total of 2,018,200 soldiers whose nativity is thus established, out of the 2,500,000 in the Union army.

Part of the war's unwritten history for the Union is the result of the firm stand the Germans took in defense of their new homeland. In the East, and still more in the West, before the Rebellion, the German element was hardly appreciated by the mass of the people. With the outbreak of the war, it asserted itself and won a place in the consideration of their fellow-citizens that has been shown by their recognition in its government and, to a still greater degree, in its social development. In the Southwest, notably, the Southern element was antagonistic to the Germans—their industry, their frugality, their sobriety, their simple tastes, their love of family, their pride in their homes, were all elements of a civilization unknown in that part of the country. When the Germans answered the appeal to support and defend the Union, their uprising was a surprise. Politicians looked unkindly at their military organizations and were indisposed to give them a place in the army. The steadiness of Blenker's division at Bull Run gave his German regiments a consideration which stood them in good stead later on when disasters befell them at Chancellorsville and Gettysburg. In the West, Sigel organized the German regiments and helped to save Missouri to the Union.

The Germans who had been soldiers at home, but were employed peacefully throughout the country, at the first appeal to arms hurried to join their fellow-countrymen, and many others joined them who had recently come over here to seek their fortunes, and not a few whose trade was war helped to swell the strength of the German regiments. Asboth organized a cavalry brigade, which did good service to the end. The 4th (German) Missouri Cavalry was one of his regiments. Although its colonel and its adjutant were Americans, most of its officers and all of its rank and file were Germans, old soldiers, who soon showed their capacity to adapt the lessons of their old military experience to the new problems of the war in this country.

The scattered settlements of Germans throughout Missouri made the strength of the Union men of that state and kept it in its place.

Encouraged in turn by their countrymen's success, large numbers of new settlers followed their example, among them many who had seen the future wealth of the country even in a time of war and that the desolating border war which carries so much misery in its course. Throughout Western Missouri, there are thriving villages and prosperous towns, connected by a network of well-tilled farms, where German is the universal element. To them, the success of the Union cause was the guarantee of their future prosperity, and from their support, it derived much of its best strength.

Colonel Waring's attractive little book, *Whip and Spur* (Boston, 1875), gives an admirable sketch of life in the 4th Missouri Cavalry. Full of grace, charming in tone and spirit, told with the true feeling of a real soldier, it shows with much more vivid truth than most professed histories the real inner life of a cavalry regiment largely made up of old German soldiers. From its lieutenant-colonel, Von Helmrich, for twenty-eight years a cavalry soldier in Germany, down to the Swiss trumpeter, all were imbued with that military spirit which makes the typical German soldier. Colonel Waring's story is one of rough campaigns, hurrying expeditions, hair-breadth escapes, soldier's life in border warfare, and it will preserve the fame of the 4th Missouri Cavalry when the dull records of many other regiments have been forgotten. It is just such a book as will serve to keep alive the best memories of the German cavalrymen in the War for the Union in the West.

The German soldier of the West and Northwest at once took his rightful place in the army and won for himself and his countrymen the respect and the affection and the confidence of his native-born fellow-citizens. What was before scanty permission has now become a matter of right, and the German, as a factor in both the country's political and social progress, owes his place to what has done and won for it in the War of the Rebellion. Many Germans undoubtedly came over here as a sort of freebooters, attracted by the high pay and the rapid promotion and all the advantages that a volunteer army enjoyed over the great standing army of their native country. When the war was over, many of them settled here and became good and useful citizens, ready to do their share in making their new homes prosperous and happy. Thus, whatever their sacrifices—and they were great in life and health—their reward has been proportionately great. The Germans throughout the civilized world owe much of their present position, of the accepted greatness of the empire, to the devotion, freely offered, of their services to the United States in its hour of trial. To the example, they then gave of fidelity to their political principles.

The story of the German soldier in the Rebellion is one of the characteristic features of that varying struggle. At the outset in the East, the German population's enthusiasm in their support of the Union was heartily welcome. In Missouri, under Sigel, it was their uprising that saved that state to the Union, and from the Germans of Missouri and the Northwest, there came soldiers who won the day against the disloyal government of the state. Fremont rallied around him bodies of German troops of a strange sort at first, but that later on in the war became useful soldiers. In New York, Blenker raised a regiment that soon swelled to a brigade, then to a division, and might have become an army corps. Their steadiness in protecting the retreat at the first Bull Run won for them general applause. During the preparation that McClellan gave his raw troops, their camp in front of Washington was a scene of military displays in the fashion of Germany, little known or appreciated by our work-a-day army but largely admired by spectators from far and near.

The German troops' successive ill-fortune under Sigel in the valley of Virginia and under Howard at Chancellorsville and Gettysburg was fully atoned for by their share in Sherman's operations. From being overpraised at the outset, they were afterward unjustly over-blamed, and the truth undoubtedly rested between the two extremes. There were incompetent officers and inefficient soldiers in their number at the outset. These were gradually weeded out, and in the end, it can fairly be said that the German soldiers in the Rebellion contributed largely to the success that finally crowned the war. To give a detailed account of so large a number, scattered over such an extent of country, would be impossible, but a few shining examples may serve the purpose.

In a pamphlet issued by the War Department in 1885, there is given the local designation of volunteer organizations in the United States Army during the War of the Rebellion, 1860-65, which is of interest, as showing in part the nationality of troops.

In New York:

- Dickel's Mounted Rifles, 4th New York Cavalry.
- Blenker's Battery, 2nd Battery Light Artillery, New York.
- Steuben Regiment, 7th New York Infantry.
- 1st German Rifles, 8th New York Infantry.
- United Turner Rifles, 20th New York Infantry.
- 1st Astor Regiment, 29th New York Infantry.
- 5th German Rifles, Forty-fifth New York Infantry.
- Fremont Regiment, Forty-sixth New York Infantry.
- Sigel Rifles, or German Rangers, Fifty-second New York Infantry.
- Barney Rifles, or Schwartze Yäger Regiment, Fifty-fourth New York Infantry.
- Steuben Rangers, Eighty-sixth New York Infantry.

In Pennsylvania:

- 1st German Regiment, Seventy-fourth Pennsylvania Infantry.
- 2nd German Regiment, Seventy-fifth Pennsylvania Infantry.

In Ohio:

- 1st German Regiment, 28th Ohio Infantry.
- 2nd German Regiment, 37th Ohio Infantry, Colonel Siber.
- 3rd German Regiment, Sixty-seventh Ohio Infantry, Colonel Burstenbinder.

In Indiana:

- 1st German Regiment, 32nd Indiana, commanded, successively, by Willich, Von Trebra, and Erdelmeyer.

In Illinois:

- Hecker's Yäger Regiment, 24th Illinois.

In Wisconsin:

- 1st German Regiment, 9th Wisconsin.
- 2nd German Regiment, 26th Wisconsin.

Bates's *History of the Pennsylvania Regiments, etc., in the Rebellion* is a huge work of five enormous volumes. There is much material to be gathered bearing on the German element in the war from its endless pages. Pennsylvania naturally claims for its citizens of German descent, including those whose ancestors were among the early settlers, a place in any tribute to the German soldiers. Among the first five companies organized in Pennsylvania at the very outset, there were many Pennsylvania Germans; and of the twenty-five regiments raised for the three months' service, there were the 4th, with Hartranft as its colonel, from Norristown and Pottstown; the 8th, from Lehigh and Northampton; the 9th, from Chester and Delaware, with Pennypacker; the 10th, from Lancaster; the 11th, from Northumberland; the 14th, from Berks; the 15th, from Luzerne; the 16th, from York and Schuylkill; the 18th, in Philadelphia, under Wilhelm; the 21st, under Ballier, largely made up of Germans.

Of the three-year regiments, those who bore the brunt of the war, there was the 27th, which gained credit from and for Bushbeck; while of the fifteen regiments of the Pennsylvania Reserves, the largest organized force, indeed the only division sent by one state to the field, many of its members were Germans by birth or descent—and so, too, of the Forty-eighth, from Schuylkill; the Fiftieth, from Berks; the Fifty-first, under Hartranft, from Montgomery; the Fifty-sixth, under Hoffman; the Sixty-fifth, better known as the 5th Cavalry; the Seventy-fourth, from Pittsburg; the Seventy-fifth, under Bohlen; the Seventy-ninth, from Lancaster; the Eighty-eighth, from Berks and Philadelphia, with General Louis Wagner; the Ninety-sixth, from Schuylkill; the Ninety-seventh, under Pennypacker, from Chester and Delaware; the Ninety-eighth, the old 21st reorganized, under Ballier, thoroughly German in rank and file;

the One Hundred and 12th, or 2nd Artillery—so large a regiment that out of it a second regiment was organized; the One Hundred and 13th, or 12th Cavalry, and the One Hundred and Fifty-second, or 3rd Artillery—almost distinctively German. Then there were the One Hundred and 30th, from York; the One Hundred and 31st, from Northumberland; and the One Hundred and Fifty-third, from Northampton—it was brigaded under Sigel, Stahel, and Von Gilsa, with the New York regiments of Salm, Holmstedt, and Von Amsberg, and the 82nd Illinois, of Hecker—nothing could point more conclusively to the German element in the war than such names as these.

The One Hundred and Sixty-eighth Pennsylvania Volunteers, from Berks, was organized and commanded by Charles A. Knoderer.

This is a fair proportion of the two hundred and fifteen regiments, nine batteries, two independent companies, and eleven colored regiments raised in Pennsylvania, and even a hasty glance at the long list of names of officers and men of the successive regiments will show a large German element scattered throughout them. One of the best elements of the little regular army was the supply of excellent non-commissioned officers, largely old German soldiers. It was a great stroke of good fortune when a volunteer company had one of these well-trained and well-disciplined men in its ranks—he steadied the whole line and gave it an example of soldierly excellence in every particular.

Such a man was Edward Scherer, first sergeant of Company B, of the One Hundred and 21st Pennsylvania Volunteers—a German who had served in a battery of the 3rd United States Artillery, under some of the most distinguished officers of the regular army. Such men as Reynolds and Burnside recognized him as an old comrade. His bearing and gallantry and knowledge of the real business of soldiering were the objects of universal admiration among the green hands, both officers and men, of his regiment. He fell at the Battle of Fredericksburg, Virginia, and he was but a type of that large number of German soldiers who served in the ranks and who, like Scherer, sacrificed good employment at home to do their duty to the country of their adoption at its hour of supreme peril and trial.

A characteristic and distinguished example of the services rendered by our Pennsylvanians of German descent is the brilliant career of General G. Pennypacker, of the 9th and the Ninety-seventh Pennsylvania Volunteers. Born in 1842 at Valley Forge, he was one of the descendants of Heinrich Pannebäcker, who came to America from Germany before 1699 and settled on Skippack Creek. Many of this family settled in the adjoining counties of Montgomery, Chester, and Berks. Of the later generations, not a few found their way into Virginia, Kentucky, Tennessee, and Mississippi, where their names are found in positions of importance and trust.

On the rolls of those who served in the Revolution and the Republic's later wars, there are many representatives of this old German stock. The Pennypacker war record is a notable one. During the Revolution, this family had as its representatives in the Continental Army a captain, an ensign, a lieutenant, a corporal, and a private. In the War of 1812, it had two of its members in the field; in the Mexican War, three. In the War of the Rebellion, it furnished to the Union army two major-generals, one adjutant-general, one colonel, one surgeon, one assistant surgeon, two captains, one lieutenant, five sergeants, eight corporals, one musician, and sixty-five privates. To the Southern army, it gave one lieutenant-colonel, one quartermaster, four captains, five lieutenants, and twenty-eight enlisted men—a total of one hundred and twenty-eight. No doubt this list could be increased if all branches of the old stock reported their military contingent. At all events, it is worth pointing out that others may try to parallel it by a diligent search through their records for other examples of the kind. The great-grandfather of General Pennypacker was a bishop of the Mennonite Church; his father was on General Worth's staff in the Mexican War. After he had begun life as a printer at the age of eighteen, young Pennypacker became a member of a local volunteer company and marched with it to Harrisburg on the first summons for troops in 1861, serving with it in the 9th Regiment. He soon became captain and then major of the reorganized regiment in the three years of service, the Ninety-seventh, and bravely fought his way through the war, became colonel of the regiment, was soon put in command of a brigade, won his star as a brigadier-general for his gallantry at the capture of Fort Fisher, at twenty-two was the youngest general officer in the war and was brevetted a major-general. In 1866 he quietly settled down to study law, when he was appointed colonel of the 34th Infantry in the regular army, then assigned to the 16th; he was the youngest colonel in the regular army, and finally retired in 1883 at an age when with most men a career of distinction such as his is usually just beginning.

Zinn, of the One Hundred and 30th; Schall, of the Fifty-first, one of eight brothers in the army; Brenholz, of the Fiftieth; Gries, of the One Hundred and 4th; Kohler, of the Ninety-eighth, were all of Pennsylvania birth, but of German descent. Knoderer, of the One Hundred and Sixty-eighth, was born in Baden, was educated at Carlsruhe, at the Polytechnical School, and left the service of the government to join Sigel's force in the unsuccessful revolution of 1849. In Reading (Pennsylvania), he found a new home and employment as a civil engineer. When the Rebellion broke out, he went first as a captain of engineers on Sigel's staff, then enlisted as a private and was elected colonel of the 11th Pennsylvania, and afterward was appointed colonel of the One Hundred and Sixty-eighth Pennsylvania and fell at its head on January 30, 1863, near Suffolk, Virginia.

Ballier was born in Württemberg in 1815; studied at the Military School at Stuttgart in 1833 to 1834; settled in Philadelphia, where he was a member of the Washington Guard, the first German military organization in the North, in 1836; enlisted as a private in the 1st Pennsylvania for the Mexican War, was made major for his services there—then was colonel of the 21st and the Ninety-eighth for the Rebellion. Twice seriously wounded, he remains with us to renew the recollection of his varied experiences, a veteran of many battles.

Hartranft's commission as brigadier-general was won by his services at Bull Run, Antietam, Fredericksburg, and as the hero of Fort Stedman, he became a major-general. His services in civil life have been equally distinguished, and his career is marked by well-earned honors, as Governor of Pennsylvania, as the chief representative of the Federal Government in Philadelphia, and as the head of the state militia.

Everard Bierer, colonel of the One Hundred and Seventy-first Pennsylvania, was the son of German parents, settled in Fayette County. He won his first successes in the 11th Pennsylvania Reserves, was appointed by Governor Curtin to be colonel of the One Hundred and Seventy-first, and was promoted to the command of a brigade. Now he is a successful lawyer, legislator, and farmer in Kansas.

Colonel Lehmann, of the One Hundred and 3rd, was born in Hanover in 1812, was educated there at the military school, served for six years in the army, and in 1837 came to Pittsburg, where he became a teacher. He organized the Sixty-second Pennsylvania, was its lieutenant-colonel, then was colonel of the One Hundred and 3rd. After the war resumed his work of education and became president of the Western Pennsylvania Military Academy.

The Wistars who served in the war by the half a score were all of that good old German stock whose representatives are so well and honorably known in every walk of life in their native city and far beyond it.

Philadelphia sent General Isaac J. Wistar, colonel of the 71st Pennsylvania; Major Joseph W. Wistar, of the 8th Pennsylvania Cavalry; Colonel Francis Wistar, captain of the 12th United States Infantry, and colonel of the Two Hundred and 15th Pennsylvania; Colonel Langhorne Wistar, captain of the 1st Pennsylvania Rifles, "Bucktails," colonel of the One Hundred and Fiftieth Pennsylvania, and brevet brigadier-general; Colonel William Rotch Wistar, of the 20th Pennsylvania Cavalry.

William Doster, colonel of the 4th Cavalry, was born in Bethlehem, Pennsylvania, where his father, a native of Swabia, settled in 1817, marrying the daughter of a Vorsteher of the Brethren's House, the granddaughter of a Revolutionary soldier. A graduate of Yale of 1857 and the Harvard Law School of 1859, he studied law in Heidelberg and Paris. Returning to this country, he became major of the 4th Pennsylvania Cavalry, led it in the Chancellorsville and Gettysburg campaigns, and was promoted for his services.

General J. William Hofmann, colonel of the Fifty-sixth Pennsylvania, was the son of Prussian parents, who settled in Philadelphia in 1819. Long an active member of local militia organizations, he went to the field a thorough soldier, and his career was one of distinguished gallantry, characterized alike by merit and modesty. The opinion of all his superior officers was an unbroken and unanimous approval of his ability and courage, and he deserves, as he has won. He enjoys the respect of his fellow-citizens for the distinguished services he rendered in all the responsible positions assigned him during his long period of active service.

General Adolph Bushbeck was born in Coblenz, Prussia, in 1822, the son of a German officer. From his eleventh to his seventeenth year, he was at the cadet school in Berlin, then became ensign and lieutenant. At the suggestion of Steinwehr, he was appointed instructor at the cadet school at Potsdam from 1847 to 1852. In 1853 he came to Philadelphia and was well and favorably known as a successful teacher. When the Rebellion broke out, he became major and later colonel of the 27th Pennsylvania, and in that and his successive commands, as general of brigade and division, won unstinted praise for his high soldierly qualities. From General Sherman, he received warm commendation. The war over, he returned to Philadelphia and resumed his former occupation for some years, and then, going abroad with his family, died in Florence, Italy, in 1883.

Henry Bohlen was born in Bremen in 1810. As early as 1831, on Lafayette's recommendation, he was appointed on General Gerard's staff and served during the siege of Antwerp. In the Mexican War, he served on General Worth's staff and took part in many engagements. In the Crimean war he served in the French army, and at the outbreak of the Rebellion, returning from Europe, where he was living in great splendor, enjoying a large fortune and a brilliant social position, he raised the Seventy-fifth, a German regiment, mainly at his own expense, and led it with such distinguished gallantry that he was commended in warm terms by Fremont and Sigel, under whom he served, and was soon appointed a brigadier-general. His brilliant career ended in his death in action in August 1862.

The Vezins—Oscar, Henry, Alfred—served with credit in various branches of the service, always doing honor to a name that belongs to one of the oldest merchants of Philadelphia in its days of greatness as a commercial city.

Henry Vezin was captain Company G, 5th Pennsylvania Cavalry; Alfred, captain Company C, 15th Pennsylvania Cavalry, and afterward adjutant 4th Missouri Cavalry.

The name of General John A. Koltes is perpetuated in that of the Post No. 228 of the Grand Army of the Republic, which thus does due honor to that gallant soldier. He organized the Seventy-third Regiment, originally known as the Pennsylvania Legion, Forty-fifth of the line. In June and July 1861, it was recruited in Philadelphia and was first at a rendezvous at Lemon Hill. Colonel Koltes, Lieutenant-Colonel Muehleck, Major Schott were the field-officers. It joined Blenker's division in September and went with it through the West Virginia campaign under Fremont and Sigel and then under Pope into the second Bull Run. Koltes was in command of the brigade and Brueckner of the regiment when they both fell in action on the 30th of August, 1862, gallantly leading their men against an overwhelming force. In his report as division commander, General Schurz commends the conduct of Koltes and his brigade, temporarily attached to his division. It consisted of the Sixty-eighth New York, the 29th New York, and the Seventy-third Pennsylvania, with Dilger's Battery. He says, "The gallant Koltes died a noble death at the head of his brave regiments," and he deplores "the brave and noble Koltes." General Sigel, who commanded the 1st Corps, regrets, in his report, "the death of the intrepid Koltes."

General Koltes was born in Treves in 1827 and came to this country while still a lad in his seventeenth year. He became a teacher in a Catholic institute in Pittsburgh, enlisted in 1846 as a volunteer in the Mexican War and afterward in the regular army. On his return, he was employed in the United States Mint, became a member of the Scott Legion, and took an active part in the local militia. He drilled the Männerchor Rifle Guards for home service and recruited a regiment for the war. He received a commission as brigadier-general, and it was at the head of his brigade that he fell in action at the second Bull Run. Koltes was, like Ballier, Binder, and Bohlen, one of the active spirits in the early military organizations in Philadelphia. Besides the Philadelphia regiments, they furnished for the war four companies of Philadelphia Turners, who joined their comrades in the Turner Regiment, organized in New York under Colonel Soest. Many went into New Jersey regiments and those of other states.

Among the young Germans of Philadelphia, Fritz Tiedeman has a high place for his gallant services. He was, successively, quartermaster-sergeant, second lieutenant, adjutant, and captain of the Seventy-fifth Pennsylvania, and then on the staff of General Schurz; and his brother, who fell early in the war, gave promise of equal merit.

General Louis Wagner was born in Giessen, Germany, in 1838, and came to Philadelphia as a lad with his father, a revolutionary refugee, in 1849. Educated at the public schools, in 1861, he entered the service as a first lieutenant of the Eighty-eighth Pennsylvania Volunteers, and at the close was colonel of the regiment and a brevet brigadier-general. Returning to civil life, he organized the Grand Army of the Republic in Pennsylvania in 1879 and has been one of the leading men of that organization ever since. He has taken a very active part in other civil and military bodies. He has been honored by many elective offices and appointments, all of which he has filled with characteristic zeal and energy.

New York, as the gathering place of all nationalities, naturally sent many Germans to the army. The 39th, or Garibaldi Guard, consisted of three companies of Germans, three of Hungarians, one each of Swiss, Italians, and French, and one of Spanish and Portuguese.

The 7th Regiment Infantry, New York State Volunteers, or "Steuben Rangers," organized by Colonel John E. Bendix, and reorganized by Colonel G. von Schach, had, as its original officers, Lieutenant-Colonel Edward Kapff, Major C. Keller, and Captains Goebel, Boecht, Brestel, Pfeiffer, Anselm, Hocheimer, S. L. Kapff, Schonleber, Bethan, Wratislau.

The 8th, or "1st German Rifles," was organized by Blenker, who commanded a brigade at the first Bull Run and a division under Fremont in the valley campaign. It was in Sigel's corps in the Second Battle of Bull Run.

The 20th, or "United Turner Rifles," was organized by the New York Turn-Verein, in April 1861, from its societies. German citizens provided the money for its expenses; a committee of ladies, called the

"Turner-sisters," supplied many necessaries. Max Weber was its colonel, Franz Weiss lieutenant-colonel, and Englebert Schnepf major.

The 29th, or "Astor Rifles," was organized by Steinwehr, who, in his farewell order, says it was the last to leave the field at Bull Run, and served with distinction under Fremont, Sigel, and at Chancellorsville, and earned a place in the history of the war.

The 5th New York State Militia was a German organization—its officers were Colonel Schwarzwalder, Lieutenant-Colonel Burger, Major von Amsberg.

Of the 41st or De Kalb Guards, Colonel von Gilsa, seven hundred of its men had been in the Prussian service in the Schleswig-Holstein war. One company was raised in Philadelphia, and another in Newark, New Jersey.

The 52nd Regiment Infantry, New York State Volunteers, was organized at Staten Island, New York, in the autumn of 1861, by the consolidation of four companies of the "Sigel Rifles," and six companies of the "German Rangers," under Colonel Paul Frank.

The commanders of companies were:

A. Captain Charles G. Freudenberg.
B. Captain Henry L. Klein.
C. Captain Gustave Schultze.
D. Captain Oscar von Schoening.
E. Captain J. C. Messerschmidt.
F. Captain Charles Mohring.
G. Captain O.C. Garwin.
H. Captain Jacob Rueger.
I. Captain Adolphus Becker.
J. Captain Francis Benzler.

The lieutenant-colonel was Louis Kasouzki; major, Philip C. Lichtenstein.

The German ladies of New York presented a national flag, a regimental flag, and two guidons.

It formed part of the 3rd Brigade, 1st Division, 2nd Corps, was brigaded with the 57th and 66th New York, and 53rd Pennsylvania, under Sumner, French, Zook, and Frank.

At Antietam, it lost its lieutenant-colonel, Lichtenstein; at Gettysburg, its brigade commander, Zook; in the Wilderness campaign under Hancock, two gallant Germans, Count Hacke and Baron von Steuben, both officers of the Prussian army, serving as volunteers in that of the Union. Count Hacke was a brave and gentle comrade, of kind, modest, and unassuming manners, endeared to his fellow-soldiers by his manly virtues. His epitaph is written in the hearts of all who knew him as a brave and true soldier who fell in battle for a noble cause. Brigadier General Samuel K. Zook was of Mennonite descent from Tredyffrin Township, Chester County, Pennsylvania. He was mortally wounded on the second day at Gettysburg while advancing in the Wheatfield. Zook was a pioneer in the field of telegraphy, having lost a patent battle to Samuel Morse. He was known as a fearless leader and disciplinarian who had memorable exchanges of profanity with his friend, General Hancock. Zook was breveted to major general upon his death.

In October of 1864, the remnant of the original 52nd, five officers and thirty-five men, under Major Retzius, returned to New York. Colonel Frank, promoted to be a brigadier-general, was succeeded by Colonel Karples, and under him, the regiment was finally mustered out in July 1865. Of the two thousand eight hundred whose names appear on its rolls, only two hundred returned; thirty-four of its officers were killed or disabled during its four years of service.

The Military Order of the Loyal Legion is for the Union army what the Society of the Cincinnati was for the Revolutionary army. Its records preserve and perpetuate the memories of many gallant soldiers. Among them is to be found a sketch of the life and services of Carl Gottfried Freudenberg. Born in Heidelberg, Germany, on May 1, 1833, he entered the military service as a cadet in the Carlsruhe School at an early age. While there, the revolution of 1848 broke out, and although but fifteen, he took the field with his fellow students and was engaged in the battle fought near Mannheim. As his mind matured, it developed such conclusions upon political liberty as compelling him to forego brilliant prospects of preferment. He came to the United States a few years before the great Rebellion. When a call was issued for soldiers, he raised a company of infantry, and with it, entered the service as captain of the Fifty-second New York Volunteer Infantry, August 3, 1861. On the 9th of November, he became its major and was severely wounded at the Battle of Fair Oaks. On November 24, 1862, he was promoted lieutenant-colonel and commanded his regiment at Chancellorsville and Gettysburg, where he was again desperately wounded. Forced to leave the field by his injuries, he resigned his commission in the Fifty-second New York and accepted an appointment as major in the Veteran Reserve Corps, organized the 23rd Regiment, and on April 22, 1864, became its lieutenant-colonel, serving in the Bureau of Refugees, Freedmen, and Abandoned Lands, as commandant at Milwaukee, as inspector-general and commandant of the District of Wisconsin. On the army's reorganization, he was appointed captain of the Forty-fifth (Veteran Reserve) Infantry; in 1869, he was transferred to the 14th Infantry, was brevetted colonel of volunteers, and as major and lieutenant-colonel of the regular army. In May 1870, he went with his regiment to the Northwest to quell a threatened Indian outbreak, but in December, he was obliged to go on the retired list as captain, and in 1877 he was promoted lieutenant-colonel. He died in Washington, August 28, 1885, enjoying the confidence and affection of all who knew him as the very embodiment of personal honor and soldierly virtue.

One of the most effective services rendered the cause of the Union was the long series of political cartoons furnished to *Harper's Weekly* during the Civil War by Thomas Nast, born on the Rhine in 1840. His pencil was recognized far and wide as that of a sturdy champion, and the soldiers heartily welcomed his productions in the field and by earnest patriots everywhere. Thomas Nast was born in Landau, Bavaria, September 27, 1840, and came with his mother to New York in 1846, and was there joined in 1849 by his father, who had served on the man-of-war "Ohio." He began to work on Frank Leslie's illustrated paper, studied in the Academy of Design, made a campaign with Garibaldi in 1860, sending sketches to the New York, London, and Paris illustrated papers, returning to New York in 1861. His contributions to *Harper's Weekly* became historical and have received the well-merited praise of historians and art critics. They were useful in keeping alive the loyal feeling of the North and received the hearty plaudits of the soldiers in the field. When peace was restored, he won new honors in the civil contest that waged over Andrew Johnson's administration, and even now, he fights for good government with his pencil.

In her book, *Ten Years of My Life*—and a very adventurous one it was—The Princess Salm-Salm describes the camp of the German division (Blenker's) in front of Washington in the fall of 1861 as the principal point of attraction. It consisted of about twelve thousand men, under Blenker and Steinwehr, who had gained great credit for protecting the retreat from the First Bull Run. Blenker was born in Tours, served in the Bavarian army and in that of Greece under its Bavarian king, took part in the German revolution of '48, fled to Switzerland, then came to New York and was farming when the Rebellion broke out. He raised the 8th New York, and Prussian and Austrian soldiers furnished a considerable proportion of its officers, among them Prince Salm-Salm, who served to the end of the war, then in Mexico, and finally fell in the Franco-Prussian war. Another of his officers was Corvin, who, after six years in Prussian prisons as a penalty for his share in the German revolution, came to this country as the war correspondent of the London *Times* and the Augsburger *Allgemeine Zeitung*.

Among other German officers were von der Groeben; von Schack, colonel of the 7th New York; von Buggenhagen, one of its captains; von Radowitz, Schwenke, Gerber, Max Weber; Schirmer, chief of artillery of the 11th Corps; von Puttkammer, of the 3rd Corps; von Amsberg, von Gilsa, von Kusserow, von Kleisser; von Schrader, of the Seventy-fourth Ohio, killed in action; von Trebra, of the 32nd Indiana; and Leppien, lieutenant-colonel of the 1st Maine Artillery, one of the most gallant soldiers from Philadelphia.

Carl Schurz was the first colonel of the first regiment of volunteer cavalry duly authorized to be raised. On his way to New York, he found

Chorman's Rangers also inviting recruits, while other cavalry companies were being busily raised in Philadelphia. In New York he found additional countrymen at work—Frederick von Schickfuss, August Haurand, Count Haake, von Blankenburg, Bern de Tavergnier, von Strautz, von Veltheim, Count Ferdinand Storch, and Count von Moltke, Hendricks, Passegger, Hertzog—who soon found plenty of men. Schurz himself went to Spain as minister, and the regiment was fortunate in having for its first colonel in the field A. T. M. Reynolds, a very good, experienced soldier. The four companies of Germans were all old soldiers. Their record through the war is a very creditable one, and the 1st New York Cavalry did its work so well that Germans may be proud of their countrymen in it both from New York and Pennsylvania.

The German element in the cavalry and artillery went far to make both of these arms of the service efficient and capable. In every regiment of cavalry and every battery of artillery, there were found old German soldiers, trained in a way that made them models for the green recruits and instructors alike of officers and men. In most of the regular army regiments, there were privates and non-commissioned officers, Germans by birth and soldiers by training, who were looked on with the respect that courage and discipline always secure. Many of them were promoted to commissions, and some of them commanded volunteer regiments with great credit. One of the most notable trained and veteran German soldiers was Adolph von Steinwehr, born September 25, 1825, at Blankenburg in Brunswick. His father was a major, his grandfather a lieutenant-general. He studied in the military school, became a lieutenant, came to the United States, and served as an officer of an Alabama regiment during the Mexican War. He was employed as an engineer by the United States, married in Mobile, returned to Germany, and then became a farmer in Connecticut. At the outbreak of the Civil War, he became colonel of the 29th New York, part of the Germans that excited interest and admiration by their steadiness at the First Bull Run. This led to the organization of a German division under Blenker—the 1st Brigade under Stahel: the 8th, Wutschel; 39th, D'Utassy; and Forty-fifth, von Amsberg, New York; and 27th Pennsylvania, Bushbeck; 2nd Brigade, Steinwehr: 29th, Kozlay;

Fifty-fourth, Kryzanowsky; Fifty-eighth, Gellman, New York; Seventy-third Pennsylvania, Koltes; 3rd Brigade, Bohlen: Forty-first, Von Gilsa, and Sixty-eighth New York, Kleefisch; Seventy-fourth, Schimmelpfennig; Seventy-fifth, Pennsylvania, Mahler; 4th New York Cavalry, Dickel; batteries of Schirmer, Wilderich, and Sturmfels. There were changes in the organization in which Sigel and Schurz obtained successive commands. Finally, at Chancellorsville, the tide turned, and the Germans of the 11th Corps were spoken of as if the ill-fortune of the battle was due to them. Steinwehr was always honored for his troops' conduct, and at Gettysburg again, his military reputation was enhanced by his services. Under Sherman, he won fresh honors in the West and served in the army until the war's end. From that time until he died in 1877, he was engaged in the work of authorship on subjects for which his thorough training especially fitted him. Many manly qualities marked his character, and his name is an enduring example of German patriotism, soldiership, and culture.

Leopold von Gilsa, colonel of the 41st New York Volunteers, the De Kalb regiment, was a typical German soldier. Born in Prussia in 1825, the son of a Prussian officer, he served in that army, for which he was specially educated, became a major in the Schleswig-Holstein war, and soon afterward came to this country. He was peaceably employed in teaching when the Rebellion broke out. Then he organized his regiment and won for it the distinction of a thoroughly well-disciplined and capable body of good soldiers. Wounded at Cross Keys, he gained the confidence and admiration of his superiors by how he handled his regiment and the brigade and his services as chief of staff to General Sigel when he was in command of the 11th and 12th Corps. He served until 1864 when he was mustered out as colonel, although he had served as commander of brigade and division. Returning to civil life, he died in New York in 1870 due to the wounds and exposure incidental to four years of almost uninterrupted campaign life, marches, and battles. Gilsa Post, No. 264, of the Grand Army of the Republic, fitly marks by the adoption of his name the honor intended to be paid his memory by those who could best appreciate his services to his adopted country and his example of the devotion of his life to the cause in which he and his countrymen were united.

The 1st New York Battalion of Light Artillery, known as Brickel's Artillery, was composed of four batteries, all Germans—Major Brickel, Captains Dietrich, Voegelin, Knierim, and Kusserow. After Antietam, where Major Arndt, commander of the battalion, was killed, the batteries were made independent and were numbered 29th, 30th, 31st, and 32nd. The 29th was afterward consolidated with the 32nd, Captain von Kusserow. Captain Kleisser was promoted to command of the 30th, and the 31st was subsequently consolidated with the 30th. In 1865, Kusserow was appointed colonel of the 2nd Regiment of Hancock's Veteran Corps. The 29th and 32nd Batteries were consolidated with the 4th and 15th Independent Batteries but retained the number 32nd. Von Kusserow was an old officer of the Prussian army, the son of General von Kusserow. He died in Philadelphia and was buried in the presence of the German consul, Major Mergenthaler, and H. Dieck, his old comrades in arms.

Colorado had forty-two Germans in the 2nd Regiment, besides others whose nationalities are given as Austria, Prussia, Poland, Denmark, Sweden, Russia, Norway, Bohemia, Saxony, Holland, Bavaria, and Switzerland; so that even on the borders, the proportion of foreigners was a very large one.

Among the notable officers from Illinois, besides Hecker, whose memory deserves especial mention, there was General Knobelsdorff, a graduate of the military school at Culm, Prussia, who was a lieutenant in the Prussian army, joined the Schleswig-Holstein army, and came with hundreds of his comrades to the United States in 1851. He lived in Milwaukee and Chicago, and when the Rebellion broke out, organized the 24th and 44th Illinois, commanded a brigade in Sigel's corps, under Asboth, and had under him Colonel Nicholas Greusel, of the 7th and 36th Illinois, and Colonel Julius C. Raith, of the Forty-third. The 13th Illinois Cavalry was also largely a German organization.

Adolph Engelmann served in the Mexican War in the 2nd Illinois. During the Rebellion, he was colonel of the Forty-third Illinois, receiving the appointment of brigadier general as a reward.

His predecessor in the Forty-third Illinois, Julius Raith, was born in Germany in 1820, came to the United States in 1837, served as a lieutenant in the 2nd Illinois in the Mexican War, was promoted to captain, and good Democrat as he had been, was ready to serve in the War for the Union as colonel of the Forty-third—a German regiment largely organized by Gustav Körner. He fell at Shiloh in command of a brigade.

Hugo Wangelin was educated at the military school of Berlin, came to the United States in 1834, served in the 12th Missouri, under Osterhaus, and succeeded him in command of the regiment when Osterhaus was promoted, making a reputation for distinguished gallantry for himself and his German soldiers, representatives of the best elements of German emigration in the West. Wangelin took part in twenty-eight engagements and died in 1883.

Gustav Körner was a leading spirit in all German organizations in the West, both in peace and war, and his term of office as governor was marked by many events of importance.

Körner himself is a representative German, and his earnest efforts to advance German culture and engraft it on American patriotism deserve hearty recognition. His services in organizing troops and in the executive chair of Illinois are well known. His name is honorably perpetuated in his book describing the successive and successful settlement of Germans throughout the United States. He has represented his adopted country creditably abroad and is now among the veterans around whom cluster the association of all that is best, alike in German and American patriotism.

Thielemann's cavalry battalion and Hotaling's company of the 2nd Illinois Cavalry, and Stolleman's and D'Osband's and Gumbart's artillery, are among the German organizations that received frequent and always honorable mention in the history of the Western campaigns.

Gumbart's Battery, 2nd Illinois Light Artillery, was organized by Captain Adolph Schwarz, a son of Major-General Schwarz of Baden. He was severely wounded at Shiloh. The first lieutenant was M. W. Mann, now a citizen of Texas.

Friedrich Hecker is one of the names that unite Germany and America in a common love of liberty. Born in Baden in 1811, educated at Heidelberg and Munich, he became a leader of the Republican party in his native country. He was recognized as one of the master-spirits of the outbreak of 1848. To its failure, we owe the large accession of many Germans, whose part in the Union cause has become one of our history's brightest pages. His welcome to his new homeland was hearty and universal. He settled down to a quiet farmer's life in Illinois, took an active share in the work of the Republican party, enlisted at the outbreak of the Rebellion in Sigel's regiment in St. Louis, and commanded, successively, the 24th and the 82nd Illinois Volunteers, and left the field only because he was so severely wounded that he could no longer serve in the army. Like Carl Schurz, he was invited to return to Germany to take part in the organization of its unity as an empire, but his love of America and American freedom made it impossible for him to leave his home. He was a representative man among the Germans, active in all their best work in civil life, and his death, on September 22, 1881, called forth the universal expression of grief and sorrow. At his grave and afterward at the dedication of a monument to his memory in St. Louis, his old associates and his younger admirers bore testimony to the respect and affection in which Hecker's name was held. Sigel, Schurz, Körner, Thielemann, Rombauer, Stifel, Ledergerber, Englemann, and many who had fought together on both continents for Republican principles, attested the service done to constitutional liberty in Europe and America by Friedrich Hecker, and the gratitude of Germany and all Germans alike in the old and the new homeland.

Colonel Emile Frey, the Swiss minister to the United States, was an officer of Hecker's Illinois regiments, the 24th and 82nd—he volunteered, and was a lieutenant in the former and became a major in the latter, thus serving as a soldier in two republics, that of his native Switzerland and in that of his temporary home. The son of a distinguished liberal leader in the Canton of Basel, the father, was fortunate enough in his old age to see him a soldier in the American Republic and later the diplomatic representative of that of Switzerland in Washington. Colonel Frey's return to the United States was made the occasion of a hearty welcome alike from his countrymen and from his fellow-soldiers, and his well-earned reputation as a soldier in defense of the American Union was heightened by his able management of the interests of the Swiss Confederation in the United

States. The tie that unites the two republics was greatly strengthened by this marked instance of the good service rendered the Union cause by its Swiss soldiers. A sketch of a Swiss company of sharpshooters serving during the war was printed at Richtersweil, Switzerland, in 1865, under the title, *Drei Jahre in der Potomac-armee oder eine Schweitzer Schützen Compagnie im Nordamerikanischen Kriege* (8vo, pp. 228). The report made to the Swiss Confederation by its veteran General Dufour is one of the best accounts of the Federal forces at the outset. The visit of that gallant soldier is still remembered by all who met him during his stay in this country.

Iowa has preserved in the reports of the adjutant-general of the State a list of its soldiers' places of nativity. Germany, of course, has its representatives in almost every organization. In the 16th and 26th Iowa Volunteers, there were companies entirely composed of Germans, rank and file. In contrast, the 5th Cavalry was composed in part of Germans enlisted at Dubuque and Burlington for the Fremont Guards by Colonel Carl Schaefer de Boernstein, who fell in action in Tennessee in May 1862 and was mourned as a gallant soldier.

Matthes's Iowa battalion won distinction in Sherman's army. Colonel Nicholas Perczel of the 10th Iowa was also commended as an excellent soldier.

From the French colonists settled at Icaria, in Iowa, came many soldiers, among them Anton von Gaudain, who was born in Berlin, of French-Huguenot stock—the son of an army officer, and himself trained for an army officer. He came to the United States at twenty-five, edited a French paper in New York, taught school, joined the Icarian community in Icaria, served for three years in the Union army, and after the war made his home in Corning, Iowa, near a settlement of French Icarians, where he died, in 1883. He was a scholar of remarkable attainments and was beloved by all who knew him.

Connecticut had in its 6th Regiment a company of Germans from New Haven, Norwich, and Waterbury, commanded by Captain Klein, who became lieutenant-colonel of the regiment, and another, under Captain Biebel, from Bridgeport, Meriden, and New York. In its 11th

Regiment, Captain Moegling had a company of Germans from New Haven and Fairfield.

Indiana, according to the report of the adjutant-general of that State, had in its volunteer regiments 6456 Germans—not far short of the 7190 credited to the State by Dr. Gould after the war had enabled him to make a fuller comparison of figures—and a fair proportion of the 14,940 foreigners serving in and for that State, and of the 155,578 of its volunteer soldiers. Among the most noteworthy of its representative German soldiers were General August Willich and Colonel John Gerber, killed in command of the 24th Indiana at Shiloh, April 7, 1862.

A German, Albert Lange, was one of the active staff of Governor Morton and worked faithfully to enable that State to do its share successfully in the War of the Rebellion. Another German, John B. Lutz, led the Indiana forces in their resistance to Morgan's raids. The 32nd was a distinctive German regiment, organized in Dearborn, Floyd, Fort Wayne, Jefferson, and other farming districts, from the best German-American settlers.

Kentucky had many Germans among its fifty-six thousand loyal soldiers. Just as the Germans saved St. Louis and Missouri to the Union, they helped keep Louisville and Kentucky out of the Confederacy. F. Bierbower was a major of the Fortieth Kentucky. Von Kielmansegge served in cavalry commands in Missouri, Florida, and Maryland, where von Koerber was also a major of the 1st Cavalry.

Minnesota wisely preserved a list of its soldiers' nativities in the reports of its adjutant-general during the war. Company G, of the 2nd Regiment, and Companies D and E, of the 5th Regiment, were both German organizations. Henning von Minden was captain of Company A of the battalion of cavalry raised by him. Emil Munch was captain of the 1st Minnesota Light Artillery. John C. Becht, major of the 5th Minnesota, and R. von Borgersock, colonel, are among the notable German officers from this State.

Maine had as lieutenant-colonel of its 1st Artillery Regiment and captain of its 5th Battery, George F. Leppien, who had been lieutenant in a Pennsylvania battery. He was well known to Philadelphians from his residence and his connection with leading citizens of that city. Educated at a military school in Germany, he showed himself a thorough soldier in his life and his heroic death.

Michigan supplied four thousand eight hundred and seventy-two Germans out of a total of fourteen thousand foreigners, and in addition to seventy-six thousand native-born citizens, in its portion of the army. It is worth noting that Gould's estimate gives only three thousand five hundred and thirty-four.

In the eleventh and twelfth volumes of *Der Deutsche Pionier*, Cincinnati, 1879 to 1880, are published numerous contributions on the outbreak of the Civil War in Missouri, by Friedrich Schnake give in great detail the part taken by its German citizens in saving that State for the Union. The leaders of German thought and opinion in St. Louis counted many who afterward fought for their faith in the ranks of the Union army. Carl Dänzer, Theodore Olshausen, Heinrich Börnstein, and L. C. Bernays, as editors of the *Westlichen Post* and *Anzeiger des Westens*, did much to strengthen their German readers in their political views, and Friedrich Münch, Franz Sigel, Friederich Hecker, and Gustav Koerner gave their powerful help to the cause of the Union. Carl Schurz, Freiderich Hassaurek, J. B. Stallo, and others were the leading Republican orators in the war of words that preceded the appeal to arms. Emil Rothe, Egly, Brühl, and Dresel were Douglas Democrats, and Carl Rümelin was spokesman—almost without any German following—for the Breckinridge wing of the party, although the secession lieutenant-governor, Thomas C. Reynolds, was said to be really named Reinhardt, of Prague. A German, Arnold Krekel, now a judge of the United States Court, presided over the convention which forever abolished slavery in Missouri. Blair and Lyon, Schofield and Saxton, were the active representatives of the national government, but their strength came from the support of the loyal Germans. The 3rd Regiment Missouri Volunteers had Franz Sigel for its colonel, the 2nd, Henry Börnstein. Born in Hamburg in 1801, he entered the Austrian army as a cadet, served in the Italian campaign in 1822, studied medicine in Vienna, was editor, actor, and author in Germany, Austria, Italy, and France, and finally settled in St. Louis after the revolution of 1848, where he established a successful newspaper. Later on, he resumed his theatrical undertaking and then returned to Vienna, where he corresponds with English and German newspapers in Europe and America. The 4th Missouri Regiment was commanded by Nicholas Schüttsner, a native of Coblenz, a soldier in the Prussian army, and an emigrant to St. Louis in 1848. One of General Lyon's most useful allies was John J. Witzig, born in Mühlhausen in 1821; educated at Châlons, at the age of nineteen, chief engineer of the Paris Orleans Railroad, six years afterward going to Italy as chief of the construction of the Milan Turin Railroad. In 1849 he came with Cabet's Icarians to Nauvoo, where he remained until 1851 when he came to St. Louis as superintendent of a locomotive works. In 1857 became superintendent of the North Missouri, in 1859 of the Iron Mountain Railroad, remaining in its service until 1865. He died in 1872, a member of a large firm of architects and engineers. Another able ally was Captain William Jackson, commander of the German artillery company. His real name was Jacquin. Born in Metz in 1821, he came to the United States in 1834, served three years in the 2nd United States Dragoons in the Florida and Indian campaigns, was discharged in 1837, enlisted in 1839 in the 3rd Infantry, and in 1844 in the 7th, serving under General Taylor in the Mexican War. Settled in St. Louis, he organized in 1852 a company of uhlans, which was afterward changed to one of dragoons. In 1859 he became captain of the Missouri artillery company. When the war broke out, he brought his guns and his company of a hundred men—all Germans except eighteen Frenchmen and Americans—out of the rebel camp into the Union service. He was lieutenant-colonel of the 15th Missouri and captain of the 2nd Missouri Artillery. One of the captains of Sigel's regiment was Constantin Blandowsky. Born in Prussia, on the border of Russian Poland, in 1821, he was educated at the Polytechnic School in Dresden, served in the French army in Algiers, took part in various unsuccessful Polish revolutions, then fought in Italy against Austria and in the Hungarian army, came to the United States in1850, and later to St. Louis. On May 25, 1861, he died of wounds received in the attack on Camp Jackson and was buried with military honors. The work done by the German soldiers of Missouri

These statements are mere generalizations, not based on any precise information, and the best reply to them is found in the facts and names here gathered together.

Carl Schurz was born on the banks of the Rhine, became well known through his active share in the flight of Kinkel, gave up his embassy in Spain to become a general of volunteers, and became a member of Hayes's cabinet. His services as an orator before the war made his name familiar to the whole country, and his return to civil life has been marked by many evidences of popular esteem and affection. As editor of a series of books on our early German history by Kapp and Seidensticker, he has again taken the place which he has so well earned as the type of German-American citizen, equally loyal to the country of his birth and that of his adoption and his home, and alike appreciated in both.

In Nebraska, the German soldiers did good service in defense of the borders from Indians, in the 2nd Cavalry, under General Sully. In one engagement in Dakota in September 1863, the Indians, numbering two thousand warriors, were defeated, but not without a severe loss. When the regiment had served out its time, its veterans were consolidated in an independent battalion of four companies and assigned to duty on the plains with the 1st Nebraska Cavalry. In the summer of 1864, the 7th Iowa Cavalry was assigned the defense of the overland post route from Fort Kearney to the borders—the 1st Nebraska Cavalry and a company of regular cavalry continued the line and protected the country from attacks by the Indians. The raids became more frequent and bloody, and hundreds of homes were destroyed, and many settlers and their families were killed or captured. The local government organized a force of volunteers, and the War Department strengthened it by such aid as it could give, and thus the country was saved a repetition of the bloody horrors of West Minnesota. The 1st Veteran Cavalry Regiment was one-half German, and under Lieutenant-Colonel Baümer provided that it was able to cope successfully with the Indians. Almost in sight of sixteen thousand hostiles, he hanged "Black Kettle," an Indian chief, convicted by a court-martial of murder. William Baümer was born in Münster, Prussia, in 1826, was educated there at its High School, was by turns a carver and turner in wood, architect, and a railroad employee. He served three years in the 13th Infantry, saw some active service, came to the United States in 1852, worked in Cincinnati, then settled in Guttenberg, Iowa, went to Dubuque, where he established his reputation as architect and builder, then went to St. Joseph, Missouri; there he joined a German rifle company, at the outbreak of the Rebellion removed to Omaha, joined the 1st Nebraska, became its captain, served to the end of the war, and died in Omaha in 1869. His name is perpetuated by the Baümer Post, Grand Army of the Republic, of Nebraska City.

New Jersey had no distinctive German regiments, although the 3rd New Jersey Cavalry, recruited at Hoboken and Jersey City, was largely composed of Germans; but German companies were found in its regiments, notably K of the 1st, D of the 2nd, E of the 3rd, A of the 4th, and G and L of the 2nd Cavalry, and K and L of the 3rd, and Batteries B and C of the 1st Artillery.

General Mindel, colonel of the 33rd New Jersey, was a very gallant and distinguished soldier.

The 3rd New Jersey Cavalry (or 36th New Jersey Regiment) was mustered into service, February 10, 1864, as the 1st United States Hussars. Among its officers were Major Siegfried von Forstner, Captains Herzberg, Schafer, Knoblesdorf, and Stoll, Lieutenants Stulpnagel, Kramer, Siebeth, Bulow, Walpel.

Joseph Karge, formerly a Prussian officer, was lieutenant-colonel of the 1st New Jersey Cavalry, commanded the 1st Brigade of Grierson's Division of Cavalry, and is now a professor at Princeton. General Mindel commanded a brigade consisting of the One Hundred and 27th Pennsylvania, the One Hundred and 34th New York, and the 33rd New Jersey.

Among the familiar names distinguished in the Rebellion is that of the Roeblings, whose services in war have been overshadowed by their brilliant success in civil life. Yet, their share was no small one in the labors and the glories of the struggle for the Union.

Captain Sohm as an artillerist and General Karge as a cavalry officer, and Major von Forstner and Major Alstrom of the 3rd New Jersey Cavalry were among those who did special service.

Ohio has a large population of Germans in its borders, and from them have come many soldiers. In the Mexican War, Cincinnati sent three German companies, Columbus, Dayton, Hamilton, each two, and the 2nd Ohio Volunteers was called the German Regiment. It was commanded by August Moor, who had served in the Florida war, and who served again in the Rebellion. When Fort Sumter was fired on, three German infantry companies and the Washington Dragoons were on their way to Washington the day the first call for troops was issued. Two German regiments were soon organized, and more than a third of the soldiers from Ohio were Germans. There were eleven German regiments: 9th, Colonel Kammerling; 28th, Colonel Moor; 37th, Colonel Sieber; Forty-seventh, Colonel Porschner; Fifty-eighth, Colonel Bausenwein; Sixty-seventh, Colonel Burstenbinder; Seventy-fourth, Colonel von Schrader; One Hundred and 6th, Colonel Tafel; One Hundred and 7th, Colonel Meyer; One Hundred and 8th, Colonel Limberg; One Hundred and Sixty-fifth, Colonel Bohländer; 3rd Cavalry, Colonel Zahm; three batteries, Hoffman's, Dilger's, and Markgraf's. The German general officers from Ohio were Weitzel, Kautz, Moor, Ammen, von Blessing, Darr, Giese, Leister, Meyer, von Schrader, and Ziegler.

August Moor, colonel of the 28th Ohio, was born in Leipsic in 1814, came to this country in 1833, was an officer of the Washington Guard of Philadelphia. With its captain, Koseritz, they took part in the Seminole War in 1836 as lieutenant of a dragoon regiment. In the Mexican War, he rose from captain to colonel of the 4th Ohio. At the outbreak of the Rebellion, he was made colonel of the 28th Ohio, the second German regiment. He became a brigadier general as a reward for his gallant service. Von Blessing of the 37th Ohio, Degenfeld of the 26th, Aug. Dotze of the Seventy-fourth Ohio, Seidel of the 3rd Ohio Cavalry, Sondersdorff of the 9th Ohio, Tafel of the One Hundred and 6th Ohio, were among those whose services are worth remembering.

General August Willich was born in Gorzyn, in East Prussia, in 1810, of an old noble family; his father had been a captain in a hussar regiment. As a child, the son, on the death of his father, became a member of the family of Schleiermacher, the famous theologian—a connection by marriage. At twelve, he was sent to the cadet school at Potsdam. In 1828, after graduating from the military school in Berlin, he became an artillery regiment officer, and in 1841, captain. A Socialist Democrat, he learned the trade of a carpenter in his leisure hours and, leaving the service, soon took a foremost rank in the revolution of 1848. In 1853 he came to the United States with the idea of organizing a force here to lead against Hamburg and Germany. He found means of livelihood in the navy yard at Brooklyn, then was appointed to the Coast Survey, and finally became editor of the *German Republican* of Cincinnati, where he was living when the Rebellion broke out. He enlisted in the 1st Ohio, became its adjutant and major of the 9th Ohio, and later, colonel of the 32nd (1st German) Indiana; was made a brigadier-general after Shiloh, when his lieutenant-colonel, Von Trebra, became colonel of the regiment. He died on January 23, 1878.

Christopher Degenfeld was born in Germany in 1824 and trained there as a soldier. He was major of the 26th Ohio Volunteers and afterward captain of the 12th Ohio Cavalry. His severe wounds obliged him to retire, and his life was shortened by his suffering, until his death, in his fifty-fourth year, in Sandusky.

Captain Hermann Dettweiler was born in Baden in 1825 and was a soldier in its revolutionary army. He served in the 6th Kentucky until his wounds obliged him to leave the field. He died in Louisville on the 11th of September, 1878.

Battery A, 1st West Virginia Artillery, Captain Furst, of Wheeling, was composed of Germans.

Wisconsin had for its war governor Edward Salomon, born in Halberstadt, Prussia, in 1828. He came to Wisconsin in 1849, and was by turns a schoolteacher, county surveyor, court clerk, lawyer, and governor. The 9th Wisconsin was raised by Colonel—later General—Frederich Salomon. Born in Prussia in 1826, engineer, architect, and soldier in Germany, he too came to the United States. He first served in a Missouri regiment but returned to organize a German regiment in Wisconsin. His companies were, among other striking titles, The Sheboygan Tigers, The Sigel Guard, The Wisconsin Tigers, and The Tell Sharpshooters. When the colonel became a brigadier-general, the regiment was commanded by Colonel Jacobi and by Colonel Charles E. Salomon, the third and eldest brother.

Colonel Charles E. Salomon was, like the governor and the general, born in Germany in 1822. He was educated as a surveyor, served as a volunteer in the Pioniers, and in 1843 became an officer of that corps. He was employed, too, in railroad and other engineering work. In 1849 he came West; in 1850 to St. Louis, where he was elected county surveyor—defeating Ulysses S. Grant in the contest for the popular vote—county engineer, and held various other technical offices in the city's service. He organized and was colonel of the 5th Missouri Volunteers, and when it was mustered out, took command of the 9th Wisconsin, winning the brevet of brigadier-general. Returned to civil life, he was frequently employed by the United States and died on February 8, 1880.

The 26th Wisconsin was another German regiment, organized at Camp Sigel, Milwaukee, and commanded by Colonel Jacobi and General Winkler. It served in the 11th Corps and shared its varying fortunes in the East and its brilliant successes under Sherman. The 27th was also a German regiment under Colonel Conrad Krez, so were the 34th, under Colonel Fritz Anneke, and the 35th, under Colonel Henry Orff. Gustav von Deutsch commanded a cavalry company from Wisconsin, which became Company M of the 4th Missouri Cavalry. The 2nd Battery, Wisconsin Artillery, was also a German organization. The Fritz Anneke of the 34th Wisconsin was also the author of the *Zweite Freiheitsampf*, published at Frankfort-on-the-Main, in 1861.

Of the German soldiers in the Rebellion, those mentioned in these pages may well be considered typical examples. These are but a small proportion of the great number who served with equal patriotism. It is not possible in any brief way to give a detailed account of all of those who were fortunate enough to be distinguished in their special services. These pages are only a sketch of the active share taken in every part of the country by its German citizens, and perhaps some more diligent student may yet complete the picture by an exhaustive study of the subject. Imperfect as it is, with all its omissions and shortcomings, it will, however, serve to show that the Germans did their share in the War for the Union, alike in numbers, in courage, in endurance, in zeal, in all the qualities that make the good soldier and the good citizen. They may fairly point with pride to the record of their achievements and claim for them the reward of duty well done. Both those who brought with them the training, skill, and experience acquired in Germany, and those who had as part of their inheritance their national qualities, deserve to be remembered; this will have been successfully done if their names are for even a little while rescued from forgetfulness and oblivion.

There were, of course, on the surface, many Germans who rose early to a dangerous eminence, and some ended their career with anything but credit to themselves or their countrymen. These were soon thinned out by the actual experiences of real war. As they disappeared, their places were taken by men of merit, and the German soldier earned the rank which his achievements had gained for him. It was in their ranks, and as non-commissioned officers, their steadiness, courage, discipline, endurance, and other manly virtues were specially marked. Courage is not such a rare virtue, but the capacity to be a good soldier in the long and weary months of inaction, in the depression incidental to defeat, in the license that follows victory, in the trying hours of imprisonment and sickness—this was the marked characteristic of the German soldier. It shone out in those regiments and companies in which the mass was made up of impetuous and undisciplined Americans, unaccustomed to obedience and self-sacrifice. Here and there a German was found who steadied the others by his example, sometimes without a word, occasionally by a little encouragement, always by his manly and soldierly qualities. The literature of the war is largely made up of the heroic achievements of those who gained promotion and distinction, but there is also found in regimental histories and in the dry annals of State records, the occasional mention of some special gallantry of the enlisted man. The story of his part of the hardships and the successes of the war remains to be told—cannot, perhaps, in view of the vast number of soldiers, ever be fully told—but wherever the German soldier served, there he made his mark by characteristic virtues, the distinguishing traits of his nationality, in both new and old country.

The following officers of the regular army were Germans:

Adam, Emil, Alton Jägers, 1861; captain 9th Illinois, 1861; major 114th Illinois, 1865; captain 5th U. S. Cavalry, 1870.

Adolphus, Philip, Prussia; surgeon, 1861-65; Maryland

Axt, Godfrey H. T., Germany; surgeon 20th New York Volunteers; USA, 1867.

Balder, Christian, enlisted USA May 12, 1857; 1st lieutenant 25th Infantry, 1862.

Bendire, Charles, enlisted USA, 1854; captain 1st Cavalry, 1873; retired 1886.

Bentzoni, Charles, enlisted USA, 1857; colonel 56th U. S. Col. Troops, 1865; captain 25th Infantry, 1866.

Clous, John W., enlisted USA, 1857; captain 24th Infantry, 1867.

Conrad, Joseph, captain 3rd Missouri, 1861; colonel 15th Missouri, 1862; captain 11th Infantry, 1869; retired as colonel, 1882.

Crone, L. E., 22nd Massachusetts, 1861; captain 42nd Infantry, 1866; retired 1870.

Decker, Th., 4th Artillery, 1875; 2nd lieutenant 24th Infantry, 1879.

De Gress, Jacob C., captain 6th Missouri Cavalry; captain 9th U. S. Cavalry, 1867; retired 1870.

Ebstein, F. H. E., enlisted USA, 1864; captain 21st Infantry, 1885.

Eggenmeyer, A., 1st lieutenant 12th Infantry; killed June 1, 1864.

Falck, William, enlisted 1858; captain 2nd Infantry, 1866; retired 1883.

Freudenberg, C. G., captain 52nd New York, 1861; captain 14th Infantry, 1869; retired as lieutenant-colonel, 1877.

Fuger, F., enlisted 4th Artillery, 1856; 1st lieutenant, 1865.

Gaebel, F., 1st lieutenant 45th Infantry, 1866.

Gardener, Corn., 2nd lieutenant 19th Infantry, 1879.

Gerlach, William, enlisted 1856; 1st lieutenant 3rd Infantry, 1879.

Goldman, H. J., 2nd lieutenant 5th Cavalry, 1877.

Green, John, enlisted July 1, 1846; major 1st Cavalry, 1868; lieutenant-colonel 2nd Cavalry, 1885.

Grossman, F. E., 2nd lieutenant 7th Infantry, 1863; captain 17th Infantry, 1871.

Gunther, S., enlisted 1st Cavalry, 1855; captain 4th Cavalry, 1870; retired 1884.

Heger, A., surgeon USA, 1856 to 1867.

von Hermann, C. J., major A. A. D. C; captain 4th Infantry, 1866.

Hesselberger, G. A., 2nd lieutenant, 1866; 1st lieutenant 3rd Infantry, 1871.

Hoelcke, William, German army, 1849-51; British Legion in Crimea; 1st lieutenant Missouri Volunteers; 1st lieutenant 39th U. S., 1866-70.

Hoffman, Ernest F., Royal Engineers, Berlin; lieutenant Prussian army, 1844-56; captain and major Italian army; 2nd lieutenant 35th Infantry, 1867.

Hoppy, E., enlisted 2nd Artillery, 1854; 1st lieutenant 9th Infantry, 1871; retired.

Ilges, Guido, 14th Infantry, 1861; lieutenant-colonel 9th Infantry, 1871.

Johnson, Lewis, 10th Indiana, 1861; bvt. brigadier general U. S. Volunteers, 1865; captain 24th Infantry, 1869.

Kautz, A. V., 1st Ohio, 1846; 2nd lieutenant 4th Infantry, 1852; captain 6th Cavalry, 1861; colonel 2nd Ohio Cavalry, 1862; brigadier general Volunteers, 1864; bvt. major general, 1865; colonel 8th Infantry, 1874.

Keller, J. W., 6th Massachusetts, 1861; 1st lieutenant 42nd Infantry, 1866; captain retired list, 1870.

Keye, F., 2nd lieutenant 10th Infantry, 1869.

Koerper, E. A., surgeon 75th Pennsylvania, USA, 1867.

Kopp, William, 1st lieutenant Washington Territory Volunteers, 1862; 1st lieutenant 13th Infantry, 1867.

Kramer, A., 2nd Dragoons, 1857; captain 15th Pennsylvania Cavalry, 1862; captain 6th Cavalry, 1874.

Kroutinger, A. W., enlisted 2nd Infantry, 1848; captain 2nd Infantry, 1864; retired 1879.

Liedtke, F. W., 11th Pennsylvania, 1861; 2nd lieutenant 43rd Infantry, 1866; 1st Infantry, 1871.

Lockwood, T. A., 2nd lieutenant 17th Infantry, 1880.

von Luettwitz, A. H., 54th New York, 1862; 1st lieutenant 3rd Cavalry, 1874; retired 1879.

Luhn, G. L., enlisted 1853; captain 4th Infantry, 1875.

Magnitzky, G., 20th Massachusetts, 1861; captain, 1864; 2nd lieutenant 14th Infantry, 1870; retired 1871.

Mahnken, John H., 1st New York Cavalry; 1st lieutenant 8th U. S. Cavalry, 1877.

Meinhold, Charles, 3rd Cavalry, 1862; captain 3rd Cavalry, 1866; died 1877.

Merkle, Charles F., 1st lieutenant 4th Artillery, 1862.

Meyer, Martin, captain 12th Infantry, 1861.

Meyers, Edward, 2nd lieutenant 1st Cavalry, 1862; 7th Cavalry, 1866.

Michaelis, O. E., 23rd New York; captain Ordnance, 1874.

von Michalowsky, T. B., 2nd lieutenant 1st Artillery, 1861; 1st lieutenant, 1863.

Motz, John, 1st lieutenant 11th Infantry, 1847.

Orlemann, L. H., 103rd, and captain 119th New York; 1st lieutenant 10th Cavalry, 1867; retired 1879.

Patzki, J. H., surgeon 15th New York; captain asst. surg. USA, 1869.

Paulus, Jacob, 5th and 50th Pennsylvania; 2nd lieutenant 18th U. S. Infantry; captain 25th Infantry, 1873.

Phisterer, F., 2nd lieutenant 18th Infantry, 1861; captain 36th Infantry and 7th Infantry, 1869.

Rawolle, W. C., 2nd lieutenant 2nd New York Artillery, 1861; 2nd lieutenant 2nd Cavalry, 1868; adjutant, 1878; captain, 1880.

Reichmann, Carl, enlisted 1881; 2nd lieutenant 24th Infantry, 1884.

Renaldo, H. O., 2nd lieutenant 9th Infantry, 1861; 1st lieutenant, 1863.

Rendlebrock, J., enlisted 1851; 2nd lieutenant 4th Cavalry, 1862; captain, 1867; retired 1879.

Ritzius, H. P., 5th New York, 1861; major 52nd New York, 1864; 1st lieutenant 25th Infantry, 1875.

Roemer, Paul, enlisted 5th Artillery, 1858; 1st lieutenant, 1866.

Ruhlen, George, 1st lieutenant 17th Infantry, 1876.

Quentin, J. E., captain 103rd New York; 1st lieutenant 14th Infantry, 1867.

Sachs, H., 2nd lieutenant 3rd. Cavalry, 1861.

Schaurte, F. W., 2nd lieutenant 2nd Cavalry, 1862; captain, 1866.

von Schirach, F. C., 54th New York, 1861; 1st lieutenant 43rd Infantry, 1866; retired 1870.

von Schrader, Alexander, 2nd lieutenant 11th Infantry, 1866; major 39th Infantry, 1866; died 1867.

Schreyer, George, 2nd lieutenant 6th Cavalry, 1866.

Schultze, Thilo, 12th Missouri, 1865; 2nd lieutenant 14th Infantry, 1865.

Schwann, Theo., enlisted 1857; captain 11th Infantry, 1866.

Sellmer, Charles, enlisted 1854; captain 11th Me., 1862; 1st lieutenant 3rd Artillery, 1877.

Simon, Charles, 2nd lieutenant 5th Artillery, 1862; 1st lieutenant, 1866.

Smith, John E., colonel 45th Illinois; colonel 27th Infantry, 1866; retired 1881.

Smith, Thos., enlisted 1867; 1st lieutenant 15th Infantry, 1877.

Steinmetz, William R., captain and asst. surg., 1871.

Stelyes, Claus, 2nd lieutenant 4th Artillery, 1863.

Sternberg, Sig., 2nd lieutenant 27th Infantry; killed 1867.

Stiebner, Eugene; army, 1st Art. Fort Sumter, 1861; 1st New York Artillery, 1862; 3rd Pennsylvania, 1863; 16th New York, 1864; 2nd lieutenant 15th Infantry, 1865; 1st lieutenant 33rd Infantry.

Stommel, Julius, 41st New York; 2nd lieutenant 43rd Infantry, 1866; 1st lieutenant, 1869.

Syberg, Arnold, captain 11th Infantry, 1847.

Thibaut, F. W., 2nd lieutenant 7th New York, 1861; 1st lieutenant 6th Infantry, 1868.

Thies, F., enlisted 1866; 2nd lieutenant 3rd Infantry, 1873.

Urban, Gustavus, army; 2nd lieutenant 5th Cavalry; captain, 1866.

Valois, Gustavus, captain 4th Maryland, 1862; captain 9th Cavalry, 1884.

Veitenheimer, Carl, 74th Pennsylvania; 2nd lieutenant 4th Infantry; 1st lieutenant, 1866.

Vermann, Otto, 2nd lieutenant 13th Infantry, 1866.

Wagner, Henry, enlisted 1856; 2nd lieutenant 11th Infantry, 1863; captain 1st Cavalry, 1869.

Walbach, John de B., 1st lieutenant Cavalry, 1799; colonel 4th Artillery, 1842; died, 1857.

Warrens, C. N., 1st lieutenant 4th Missouri, 1861; captain 14th Infantry, 1883.

Wedemeyer, W. G., enlisted 1861; captain 16th Infantry, 1865.

Wenckebach, E. F., 2nd lieutenant 13th Infantry, 1865; captain 22nd Infantry, 1867.

Wesendorff, Max, 1st lieutenant Washington Territory Volunteers, 1862; 2nd lieutenant 24th Infantry, 1867; captain 1st Cavalry, 1880.

Wilhelmi, Louis, 2nd lieutenant 1st Infantry, 1865; 1st lieutenant, 1880.

The following, from a *List of Field Officers of U. S. Volunteers*, are Germans:

Abell, Caspar K., major 72nd New York
Abell, Charles C., major 6th New York and 10th New York Artillery
Almstedt, Henry, colonel 1st Missouri; 2nd Missouri Light Artillery
Alstrom, John V., major 3rd N. J. Cavalry
Ammen, Jacob, colonel 12th Ohio
von Amsberg, George, colonel 45th New York
Anselm, Albert, lieutenant-colonel 3rd Missouri
Arn, F., major 31st Indiana
Balling, O. H. P., major 145th New York
Banghof, C., major 1st Missouri Cavalry
von Baumbach, C., major 24th Wisconsin
Bausenwein, V., colonel 58th Ohio
Becht, John C., major 5th Minnesota
Beck, Arnold, lieutenant-colonel 2nd Missouri
Beck, Christian, lieutenant-colonel 9th Indiana Cavalry
Beck, Fred, major 108th Ohio
Beck, William, major 27th Missouri
Becker, Adolph, lieutenant-colonel 46th New York
Becker, Gottfried, lieutenant-colonel 28th Ohio
Becker, Philip, lieutenant-colonel 5th Pennsylvania Cavalry
Behlendorff, F., major 13th Illinois
Bendix, John E., colonel 7th New York
Bierbower, F., major 40th Kentucky

Blenker, L., colonel 8th New York
von Blessing, L., lieutenant-colonel 37th Ohio
von Boernstein, Shaeffer, colonel 5th Iowa Cavalry
von Borgersock, R., colonel 5th Minnesota
Botchfur, Hugo, major 1st Ark. Cavalry
Bramlich, Charles, major 2nd Ark. Infantry
Brutsche, John D., lieutenant-colonel 8th Missouri Cavalry
Burger, Louis, colonel 5th New York
Degenfeld, Christian, colonel 26th Ohio
Deitzler, George W., colonel 1st Kansas
Diechman, Julius, major 15th New York Heavy Artillery
Dotze, Aug., lieutenant-colonel 8th Ohio Cavalry
Duysing, Emil, lieutenant-colonel 41st New York
von Egloffstein, F. W., colonel 103rd New York
Ehrler, Francis, lieutenant-colonel 2nd Missouri
von Einsidel, D., lieutenant-colonel 41st New York
Erdelmeyer, F., lieutenant-colonel 32nd Indiana
Ernenwein, C., lieutenant-colonel 21st Pennsylvania
Faltz, Ernst M., lieutenant-colonel 8th Maryland
von Forstner, S., major 3rd New Jersey Cavalry
Gaebel, F. A. H., major 7th New York
Gellman, F., lieutenant-colonel 58th New York
von Gerber, G., lieutenant-colonel 6th Indiana
Glapcke, Herman, major 22nd Connecticut
Goelzer, Aug., lieutenant-colonel 60th Indiana
Gruesel, Nich., colonel 7th Illinois
von Hammerstein, H., colonel 78th New York
Happel, Christian, lieutenant-colonel 10th Missouri
von Hartung, Adolph, colonel 74th Pennsylvania
Hassendeubel, F., colonel 3rd Missouri
Heinrichs, Gust., lieutenant-colonel 4th Missouri Cavalry
Heintz, R., major 28th Ohio
Heintzleman, M. T., lieutenant-colonel 172nd Pennsylvania
von Helmrich, G., lieutenant-colonel 5th Missouri Cavalry
Hequembourg, A. G., lieutenant-colonel 40th Missouri
Hequembourg, W. A., lieutenant-colonel 3rd Missouri
Hundhausen, Julius, lieutenant-colonel 4th Missouri
Hundhausen, Robert, colonel 4th Missouri
Jacobsen, Aug., lieutenant-colonel 27th Missouri
Jaensch, F., major 31st Missouri
Jussen, Edm., lieutenant-colonel 23rd Wisconsin
Kaercher, Jac., lieutenant-colonel 12th Missouri

Kahler, F. M., major 62nd Ohio
Kammerling, Gus., colonel 9th Ohio
von Kielmansegge, E., colonel 4th Missouri Cavalry; 1st Florida Cavalry
Knobellsdorff, Charles, colonel 44th Illinois
Knoderer, Charles, colonel 167th Pennsylvania
von Koerber, V. E., major 1st Maryland Cavalry
Koltes, John A., colonel 73rd Pennsylvania
Kozlay, E. A., colonel 54th New York
Krekel, Arnold, major Missouri Battery
Kreutzer, William, lieutenant-colonel 98th New York
Krez, Cornel., colonel 27th Wisconsin
Kummell, A. H., lieutenant-colonel 13th Wisconsin
von Kusserow, C., lieutenant-colonel 2nd U. S. Veteran Volunteers
Laiboldt, Bernard, colonel 2nd Missouri
Landgraeber, Clemens, major 2nd Missouri Light Artillery
Ledergerber, F. T., major 12th Missouri
Leppien, George F., lieutenant-colonel 1st Maine Artillery
Mahler, F., colonel 75th Pennsylvania
von Matzdorff, A., lieutenant-colonel 75th Pennsylvania
Mehler, Adolph, lieutenant-colonel 98th Pennsylvania
Metternich, G., lieutenant-colonel 46th New York
Minden, von Henning, major Hatch's Battalion Minnesota Cavalry
von Mitzel, Alex., lieutenant-colonel 74th Pennsylvania
Moor, Aug., colonel 28th Ohio
Mueller, Charles, lieutenant-colonel 107th Ohio
Osterhaus, P. J., colonel 12th Missouri
Perczel, N., colonel 10th Iowa
Porchner, F., colonel 47th Ohio
Possegger, F., major 1st New York Cavalry
Reichard, F. H., major 188th Pennsylvania
Reichard, George N., lieutenant-colonel 143rd Pennsylvania
Rolshausen, F., major 82nd Illinois
Rosa, Rudolph, colonel 46th New York
Rosengarten, Adolph G., major 15th Pennsylvania (Anderson) Cavalry
Salm-Salm, Prince, colonel 8th New York
von Schach, G. W., colonel 7th New York
Schadt, Otto, lieutenant-colonel 12th Missouri
Schaeffer, F., colonel 2nd Missouri
von Schickfus, F., lieutenant-colonel 1st New York Cavalry
von Schilling, F., major 3rd Pennsylvania Art.
Schimmelfennig, A., colonel 74th Pennsylvania
Schirmer, L., colonel 15th New York

Schlittner, Nich., colonel 4th Missouri
von Schluembach, Alex., major 29th New York
Schnepf, E., lieutenant-colonel 20th New York
Schoeffel, F. A., lieutenant-colonel 13th New York
von Schrader, Alex., lieutenant-colonel 74th Ohio
Schumacher, F., major 21st Wisconsin
Segebarth, H., major 3rd Pennsylvania Artillery
Seidel, C. B., colonel 3rd Ohio Cavalry
Seidel, G. A., major 7th New York
Seidlitz, Hugo, major 27th Pennsylvania
Soest, Clemens, colonel 29th New York
Sondersdorff, C., lieutenant-colonel 9th Ohio
Stahel, Julius, colonel 8th New York
von Steinhausen, A., lieutenant-colonel 68th New York
von Steinwehr, A., colonel 29th New York
Tafel, Gust., lieutenant-colonel 106th Ohio
Tassin, A. G., colonel 35th Indiana
Thielemann, Christian, colonel 16th Illinois Cavalry
Thielemann, Milo, major 16th Illinois Cavalry
Thoman, Max, lieutenant-colonel 59th New York
Tiedemann, D. F., lieutenant-colonel 110th U. S. Colored
von Trebra, H., colonel 32nd Indiana
von Vegesach, E., colonel 20th New York
Veitenheimer, Carl, lieutenant-colonel 74th Pennsylvania
Wagner, Louis, colonel 88th Pennsylvania
Wangelin, Hugo, colonel 12th Missouri
Weber, Max, colonel 20th New York
von Wedell, Carl, major 68th New York
Willich, A., colonel 32nd Indiana
Zakrzenski, H., lieutenant-colonel 2nd Missouri

Conclusion

The Honorable Andrew D. White, lately President of Cornell University, and former United States Minister to Germany, gave an admirable summary of the intellectual debt of the United States to Germany in his address, delivered October 4, 1884, at the centennial celebration of the German Society of New York. The title is the key to the note he strikes. It is entitled "Some Practical Influences of German Thought upon the United States," and it is full of suggestive ideas and profound thoughts. He refers to the Revolution, when "the organizing power of Steuben, the devotion of Kalb, and the rude courage of Herckheimer were precious in establishing the liberties of the country;" to the recognition of the infant Republic by Frederic the Great, first of all, European rulers; and to the "earnestness of German-American thinkers, so long as the struggle was carried on with the pen, and the bravery of German-American soldiers when it was carried on by the sword." He pays fitting tribute to the words and deeds of sympathy that came from Germany alone in the fearful darkness and distress of the Civil War, when "German scholars and thinkers, men like Theodore Mommsen and his compeers, proclaimed their detestation of slavery and their hope for the American Union." In another place, he shows the reflex effect of the great work done by a German-American as orator, soldier, and statesman, when, speaking of Carl Schurz as "first of all the recent American thinkers," he tells us that Bismarck said to him, "As a German, I am proud of the success of Carl Schurz." He closes in an earnest hope that "the healthful elements of German thought will aid powerfully in evolving a future for this land purer in its politics, nobler in its conception of life, more beautiful in the bloom of art, more precious in the fruitage of character." What the Germans have already done in and for this country is the best assurance that this fervent prayer will be granted. To show their share as soldiers in the wars of the United States is at least a justification of the right and duty cast upon them to see that so far as in them lies, neither from within nor without shall any injury befall the Republic.

Afterword

by Morris Jastrow, Jr.
Originally published by the American Philosophical Society in
Proceedings of the American Philosophical Society,
Vol. 60, No. 4 (1921), pp. iii-ix

Joseph George Rosengarten, third son of George D. Rosengarten and Elizabeth Bennett, was born in Philadelphia, July 14, 1835. He received his early education in private schools of this city and for a time came under the influence of a scholarly man in York, Pennsylvania, the Reverend Charles West Thomson, who aroused in him a liking for literature that became an abiding habit and accounted for the astonishing voracity in reading that marked him to the end. He passed from the old Academy (the institution out of which grew the College and University of Pennsylvania) to the College itself and received his degree of A.B. from the University of Pennsylvania in 1852 at the early age of seventeen, and three years later the degree of M.A. After graduation he studied law in the office of Henry M. Phillips, one of the leaders of the Philadelphia Bar, and was admitted to practice in 1856. The elder Rosengarten, realizing the extraordinary value of foreign study and travel, sent four of his sons abroad to prepare themselves for their future careers. In pursuance

Joseph George Rosengarten

of this plan Joseph Rosengarten went abroad shortly after being admitted to practice, to study history and Roman law at the University of Heidelberg and to engage in travel. In this way he was thrown into contact with men of distinction in various fields and acquired that appreciation of scholarship which grew ever stronger with the passing years. Besides the eminent men at that time at the University of Heidelberg, among them Haeusser, the professor of history, and Vangerow, the professor of law, he met among others during his European studies, James Fitzjames Stephen, the great jurist, and his equally famous brother Leslie Stephen.

Returning to this country in 1857, it was not long before the rumbling of the thunder in the distance was heard. By a curious chance Mr. Rosengarten witnessed the first outbreak against slavery, the famous raid of John Brown. He happened to be traveling as a guest with the directors of the Pennsylvania Railroad (of which his father was one) on a tour of inspection. The train stopped at Harper's Ferry and there Mr. Rosengarten saw the attack made by the soldiery on the engine house in which John Brown had taken refuge. He saw John Brown lying wounded and he gave a description of the hero in a vivid article contributed by him to the *Atlantic Monthly* in 1865. May we not assume that the incident made an impression upon his youthful spirit which intensified the fervor with which he threw himself into the Union cause?

Upon the outbreak of the war, he first joined a company of volunteers, Company A of the Pennsylvania Artillery, which was made up largely of lawyers. It included men like Chief Justice Mitchell, Judges Penrose and Hanna, Mr. R. C. McMurtrie, John G. Johnson, Charles Godfrey Leland, George W. Biddle, William Henry Rawle, and among the survivors of this company are Judge Wilson, Mr. C. Stuart Patterson, and Mr. Frank Rosengarten. Later he became enrolled in the 121st Regiment, Pennsylvania Volunteers, of the Corps of the Army of the Potomac. His regiment was assigned to guard the city of Washington and subsequently passed further south. In the engagement at Fredericksburg, he distinguished himself for bravery, picking up the colors after four sergeants had been disabled and carrying them successfully through the engagement. The attention of Major General John F. Reynolds was called to the act of the young officer and he was offered the post of Ordnance Officer and a member of General Reynolds's staff. He remained with General Reynolds until the battle of Gettysburg in which General Reynolds fell. To Major Rosengarten was assigned the honor of bringing the body of the fallen hero to Lancaster. His association with General Reynolds was intimate and he was the natural selection deputed to deliver the address at the dedication of the monument to Reynolds at Gettysburg in 1889.

After the war Major Rosengarten returned to Philadelphia and resumed the practice of law in an office in which he was associated with the late George Junkin and Mr. Henry S. Hagert, both men who rose to eminence. A great part of his time was taken up with the management of his father's business affairs, for the elder Rosengarten by virtue of his unusual ability was not only a pioneer in founding and building up a large chemical establishment, but became interested in many other business ventures, and with rare foresight promoted enterprises that proved to be of value to the country as well as successful from a financial point of view.

I have not been able to ascertain when Mr. Rosengarten's participation in the work of the many public institutions with which he became connected, and with which his name will always be associated, began. In the case of the University of Pennsylvania there was no interruption in his interest from the year 1848, when he entered the college as a freshman, until his death. By the close of the seventies, we find him absorbed also in other public institutions like the House of Refuge and the German Hospital, now the Lankenau Hospital. He was elected a member of the board of managers of the House of Refuge in 1878, served as vice-president of the corporation from 1893 to 1910, and as president from 1911 to 1914. He was the assistant chairman of the board from 1893 to 1908, and the chairman from 1908 till 1914. It was largely through his urgency that the complete change in the treatment of the juvenile offenders was carried out through the removal of the institution from the city to the country, at Glen Mills for the boys, and at Sleighton Farms for the girls. Instead of being treated as prisoners the boys and girls were placed in homes organized on the cottage system. They were placed at work in the fields, given enlarged opportunities for education, and through gymnastic exercises placed in a receptive physical condition for receiving cultural influences through music and other high forms of entertainment.

Mr. Rosengarten was a close friend of the late John D. Lankenau, the great benefactor of the institution which now properly bears his name, and many of the plans for the enlargement of the hospital and the home were carried out by Mr. Lankenau in consultation with Mr. Rosengarten. He served from 1871-1913 as solicitor for the institution, and as honorary solicitor till his death.

Service on the board of a public institution was never a perfunctory performance with him. It may be said of him that he never accepted a public position without taking upon himself a conscientious spirit the duties involved. Though already heavily burdened he accepted a position as member of the board of the newly founded Drexel Institute in 1892 and served until 1909. Here again his close association with Mr. Anthony J. Drexel, who frequently talked over with him the plans of the proposed endowment, enabled him to play a particularly valuable part in bringing about the consummation of the purpose which Mr. Drexel had in mind.

Another achievement of a notable character was Mr. Rosengarten's participation in the activities of the Free Library, established in February 1891, through the efforts mainly of the late Dr. William Pepper, and prompted by a large bequest of the late George S. Pepper, which was made available for the Free Library. He was elected a member of the board in 1895 and served till 1911. For ten years from 1899 till 1909 he took upon himself the added responsibilities of president of the institution. It was largely through him that the Free Library obtained the splendid gift of one and a half millions from the late Andrew Carnegie, for the establishment of thirty branches; and it is interesting to note in this connection, as an example of the manner in which seeds of kindness take root and in due time bring forth fruit, that it was the elder Rosengarten's aid and encouragement given to the young Carnegie at the time when he acted as secretary of President Thomas A. Scott of the Pennsylvania Railroad, that proved to be a strong factor in inducing Mr. Carnegie to respond to an appeal made to him by the son of the man who had helped Mr. Carnegie in his own career.

Mr. Rosengarten's services to the University of Pennsylvania constitute a chapter by itself. From the day that he was graduated from the old college on Ninth Street, in 1852, up to his resignation as trustee in 1918, he was incessant in his efforts to help every movement looking toward the expansion of the university. There is literally no department of the university which does not bear evidence of his interest and of his generosity. At all times active in the affairs of the College Alumni Society, he served as president for many years, 1895 to 1905, and as a member of the board of managers up to a few years before his death. It was as the representative of the Alumni Society that he was elected to the board of trustees in 1896; and, in 1907, his Alma Mater paid tribute to the invaluable services rendered by her distinguished son to the nation, to research, as well as to the institution itself, by conferring upon him the honorary degree of LL.D.

Of his services to our American Philosophical Society, I also cannot speak at length without passing beyond the limits of an obituary sketch. His interest in the affairs of the Society was unceasing, from the time of his election in 1891. He served as a member of the Library Committee from 1899 to his death and as Chairman of the Committee since 1909. It is worthy of note that this position is the only one which he retained of the many which he once held, and all of which he relinquished a few years ago by virtue of advancing years which prompted him to transfer the burden to younger men. He was Councilor of the society from 1901 till 1909, and again from 1911 to 1913; and he was honored by an election to the Vice-Presidency in 1918. A perusal of the minutes will show that no one exceeded him, and few equaled him, in punctilious attendance at the meetings. He took a prominent part in the various celebrations organized by the Society, notably in the bicentennial of Franklin's birth and he is represented in the *Proceedings* by many papers, dealing with such various subjects as the French members of the Society, the Franklin Papers in the possession of our Society, the Earl of Crawford's manuscript likewise owned by our Society, the Chateau de Rochambeau, the Paris

Exposition of Books, etc. Of special value is a paper on American History from German Archives (published in the Proceedings for 1900), which gives a survey of this very fruitful field of investigation. Mr. Rosengarten himself contributed to the publication of "German Archives" by his translations of Popp's Diary and of Achenwall's Observations on North America, both published in the *Pennsylvania Magazine of History and Biography* (Vols. 26 and 27). Mr. Rosengarten's intimate association with the Society led to his being chosen to read the obituary notice of such distinguished members as Henry Coppee, William H. Furness, Henry C. Lea, J. Sergeant Price, Peter F. Rothermel, and Albert Henry Smyth. The last paper read by Mr. Rosengarten before the Society was an investigation and discussion of a "Plan for an automatic collection and distribution of a state tax for higher education." This was in 1913 and the article published in Vol. 52 of the *Proceedings* under the title of a "Counsel of Perfection" is an indication both of his thorough study of the subject of higher education and of his mature views reached after a lifetime, full of achievement on his .own part for the encouragement of higher education and for the promotion of research.

Early in life he began to write for such journals as *The North American*, *The Atlantic Monthly*, *The Penn Monthly*, the *New York Nation*, and various daily newspapers, as the *New York Tribune* and the *Philadelphia Public Ledger*. Through his association with Henry C. Carey, he became interested in social science and read largely on this subject by the side of history and literature. He was active in the establishment of the Social Science Association which later developed into the American Academy of Political Science. A field of history which appealed particularly to him was the study of the part taken by German and French immigrants in the development of this country. Besides numerous articles, addresses and papers, the fruit of his labors in this field are to be seen in two volume, *The German Soldier in the Wars of the United States*, published in 1886, and of which a second edition, revised and enlarged, appeared in 1890; and *French Colonists and Exiles in the United States*, issued in 1907. These two volumes represent contributions of permanent worth by virtue of the careful study of the material gathered by Mr. Rosengarten. In both volumes he traces the immigration of German and French settlers to their beginnings and shows exactly what influence was exerted by these elements of the population in each period of our country, down through the Civil War.

A bibliography of his papers, monographs, and books, prepared some years ago and reaching to 1907, brings the number of entries close to one hundred, and since the preparation of this bibliography Mr. Rosengarten, despite advanced years, continued to write for various journals and transactions.

No sketch, however brief, of Mr. Rosengarten's life should fail to touch on his intimate association with the scholars, writers, statesmen, men in public life in many lands, in this country, in England, France, Germany, Austria, Holland, and Italy. There were few men who had a large circle of acquaintance; and having a rare gift for friendship, he continued to maintain association with many of those with whom he was thrown into contact either in this city or through his frequent trips abroad. He knew the Darwins, father and son; he came into close touch with eminent writers and scholars like F. Max Miller, Thomas Hughes, Goldwin Smith, Herbert Spencer, and Lord Bryce; he formed a friendship extending over many years with the de Rochambeau family and secured the passage of an act of Congress for the purchase of the letters of Washington to Rochambeau. He knew the great trio of American literature, Longfellow, Emerson, and Lowell; he had met all the Presidents from Buchanan to Wilson and knew practically all the generals in the Civil War.

Mr. Rosengarten passed away quietly on January 14, 1921.